URSULA

Cross Stitch
BY THE SEA

Ursula Michael

David and Charles

www.mycraftivity.com

This book is dedicated to my children, Mark and Yvonne, who gave me the pleasure of spending countless days by the sea building chunky sandcastles, collecting assorted seashells and splashing in the cold ocean waves.

A DAVID & CHARLES BOOK
Copyright © David & Charles Limited 2009

David & Charles is an F+W Media Inc. company
4700 East Galbraith Road, Cincinnati, OH 45236

First published in the UK and US in 2009

Text and designs copyright © Ursula Michael 2009
Layout and photography copyright © David & Charles 2009

Names of manufacturers, fabric ranges and other products are provided for the information of readers, with no intention to infringe copyright or trademarks.

A catalogue record for this book is available from the British Library.

ISBN-13: 978-0-7153-2963-4 hardback
ISBN-10: 0-7153-2963-4 hardback
ISBN-13: 978-0-7153-2964-1 paperback
ISBN-10: 0-7153-2964-2 paperback

Printed in China by Donnelley Shenzhen
for David & Charles
Brunel House   Newton Abbot   Devon

Senior Commissioning Editor Cheryl Brown
Editor Bethany Dymond
Assistant Editor Kate Nicholson
Project Editor and Chart Preparation Lin Clements
Art Editor Charly Bailey
Designers Eleanor Stafford and Emma Sandquest
Photographers Kim Sayer and Karl Adamson
Production Controller Ros Napper

Visit our website at www.davidandcharles.co.uk

David & Charles books are available from all good bookshops; alternatively you can contact our Orderline on 0870 9908222 or write to us at FREEPOST EX2 110, D&C Direct, Newton Abbot, TQ12 4ZZ (no stamp required UK only); US customers call 800-289-0963 and Canadian customers call 800-840-5220.

CONTENTS

TO THE SEASIDE...

What can be better than spending a day by the sea? Some people enjoy soaking up the sun on a smooth stretch of beach; others comb the sand collecting shells while children splash in the water and build exotic sand castles. My favourite pastime is gazing at the sea. From my back porch, from a sailboat or from a rocky shore with a friend, with a cup of iced tea and a comfy chair, I never tire of the sight.

There is something about the ocean that draws us back time and time again. The never-ending sound of the waves crashing on the shore erases the mental abrasions of daily life, cleansing away our worries as they deposit sea treasures on the beach. Natural life thrives in the salty water and along the sand marshes. Coastal communities bloom with summer guests strolling on boardwalks, sailing ports filled with ships of every kind and fishermen hauling in a catch of the day. Lobster pots, ropes curled into traditional sailor's knots and squawking seagulls can be found near piers along any coastline. Colourful cottages dot the shoreline and on sunny days, vivid beach towels line up in rows on the sand while beachgoers picnic and play until a romantic sunset ushers in a night full of stars.

While some of us live by the sea, others may only escape to the seaside occasionally but the unique collection of cross stitch designs in this book will capture your favourite moments and bring back fond memories of seaside visits. The designs are varied and versatile and you will have plenty of seaside motifs to choose from. A seashell sampler and small nautical motifs may add the perfect touch to a guest bedroom. Sailboats in rainbow colours will brighten up any corner in your home. Perhaps a collection of serene sea birds or a bold lobster pillow is more your style. A stitched lighthouse picture may remind you of a wonderful get-away weekend with your loved ones. Often, a rented beach house hosts informal family events, held outdoors with tropical-themed decorations. An evening walk on the beach with a particular friend may create memories for a lifetime.

Every day the sea calls out to me; she changes with the hours and the seasons, constantly gurgling a new song and running through my veins with a salty force. I hope you enjoy your trip to the sea with my cross stitch designs as much as I have enjoyed bringing these designs to you.

'Twenty years from now, you will be more disappointed by the things that you didn't do than by the ones you did do. So throw off the bowlines. Sail away from the safe harbor. Catch the trade winds in your sails. Explore. Dream. Discover.'
(Mark Twain)

With all my heart

Cottages by the Sea

For many people, time spent by the sea is both memorable and enjoyable. Whatever your seaside dreams may be, there is always a way to enjoy a bit of heaven near the ocean and the projects in this chapter will bring it just that bit closer.

My entire life has been spent living less than an hour from the sea. When I was a child, my parents packed up the car on Sundays with picnic baskets, swimming supplies and beach umbrellas. With assorted relatives, we drove to the beach and marked our spot on the sand for the day. In later years, we rented homes by the sea and enjoyed watching a parade of watercraft sail by. We now live in a seaside community dotted with eclectic cottages and weathered mansions. Each summer the homes come to life like gift boxes decorated with colourful snips of towels, toys and beach treasures. Enjoy the sounds of summer with this delightful seaside scene and imagine the calls of birds, children's laughter and the lapping waves. Two smaller projects, a guest book and a key hanger, will also bring the seaside closer to home.

This charming scene with its collection of sweet little houses epitomizes a relaxed life by the sea, while a rustic key hanger is perfect to decorate with seaside treasures.

Sweet Retreat Picture

Step back in time to childhood days spent with the family in a tiny seaside cottage, when building sandcastles and collecting seashells was the most important thing to do.

Stitch count
135h x 180w

Design size
24.5 x 32.6cm (9¾ x 12¾in)

You Will Need

White 14-count Aida
40.6 x 48.3cm (16 x 19in)

Tapestry needle 24–26

DMC stranded cotton (floss)
as listed in the chart key

Weathered wood picture frame

1 Prepare for work, referring to page 100 if necessary. Mark the centre of the fabric and centre of the chart on pages 12–15. Mount your fabric in an embroidery frame if you wish.

2 Start stitching from the centre of the chart and fabric and work over one Aida block. Use two strands of stranded cotton for full and three-quarter cross stitches. Use two strands to backstitch the words and one strand for all other backstitches.

3 Once all stitching is complete, press the work and then finish your picture by mounting and framing (see page 102).

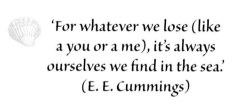

'For whatever we lose (like a you or a me), it's always ourselves we find in the sea.'
(E. E. Cummings)

Sandy Feet Key Hanger

A lucky find of scavenged wood on the beach makes a unique base to add a stitched sentiment and seashell treasures (see picture on page 7). Adding screw hooks and wire to the sign makes an inviting key rack to hang by the front door.

Stitch count
30h x 120w

Design size
5.4 x 21.6cm (2⅛ x 8½in)

You Will Need

Fiddler's Light 14-count Aida
15.2 x 35.5cm (6 x 14in)

Tapestry needle 24–26

DMC stranded cotton (floss)
as listed in the chart key

Iron-on interfacing

Driftwood to fit

Rope trim

Seashells and small pebbles

Fast-tack craft glue

Two screw hooks

Curly wire (from craft stores)

1 Prepare for work, referring to page 100 if necessary. Mark the centre of the fabric and centre of the chart on pages 10–11. Mount your fabric in an embroidery frame if you wish.

2 Start stitching from the centre of the chart and fabric and work over one Aida block. Use two strands of stranded cotton for cross stitches and one strand for backstitches. Once all stitching is complete, press the work.

3 Prepare the driftwood by cleaning any loose debris. Drill two small holes at each end and insert the curly wire for the hanger. Fuse iron-on interfacing to the back of the stitched work (see page 102) and trim around the stitching in a free-form line.

4 Glue the work to the wood and then glue a rope trim around the edges of the stitching. Knot the ends of the trim to prevent it from unravelling. Glue your seashells and pebbles in place and screw in hooks where required.

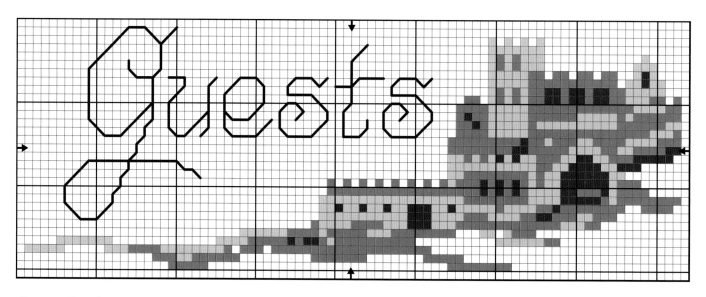

Guest Book
DMC stranded cotton
Cross stitch

■ 434

■ 436

□ 738

Backstitch

— 3842

Sandy Feet Key Hanger
DMC stranded cotton
Cross stitch

■ 321	■ 986
□ 726	■ 988
■ 826	■ 3705
■ 827	■ 3842
■ 946	▪ blanc

Backstitch

— 321

— 3842

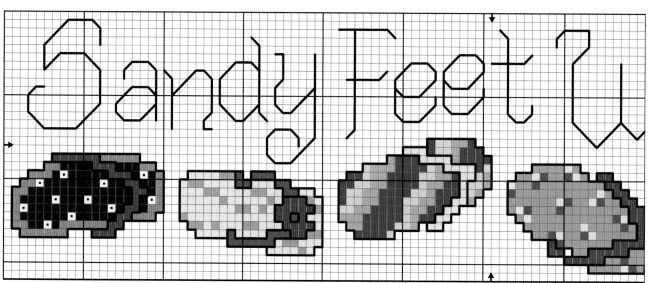

Guest Book

Guests will enjoy sharing their thoughts and reading the memories of previous guests in this handy little book.

1 Prepare for work, referring to page 100 if necessary. Mark the centre of the fabric and centre of the chart (left). Mount your fabric in an embroidery frame if you wish.

2 Start stitching from the centre of the chart and fabric and work over one Aida block. Use two strands of stranded cotton for cross stitches and one strand for backstitches.

3 Once all stitching is complete, press the work. Trim around the stitched area to fit your guest book and glue in place. Glue ric-rac trim around the raw edges of the Aida and add a bow.

Stitch count
29h x 82w

Design size
5 x 14.7cm (2 x 5¾in)

You Will Need

Rainbow/white metallic
14-count Aida (Zweigart #3706-014-59)
at least 7.6 x 20.3cm (3 x 8in)
or to fit your journal

Tapestry needle 24–26

DMC stranded cotton (floss)
as listed in the chart key

Purchased journal

Ric-rac trim and little bow

Tacky glue

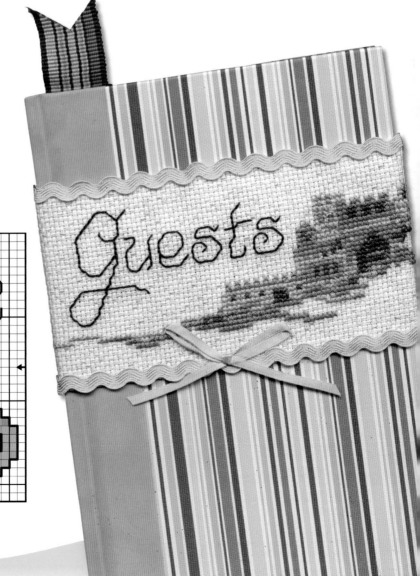

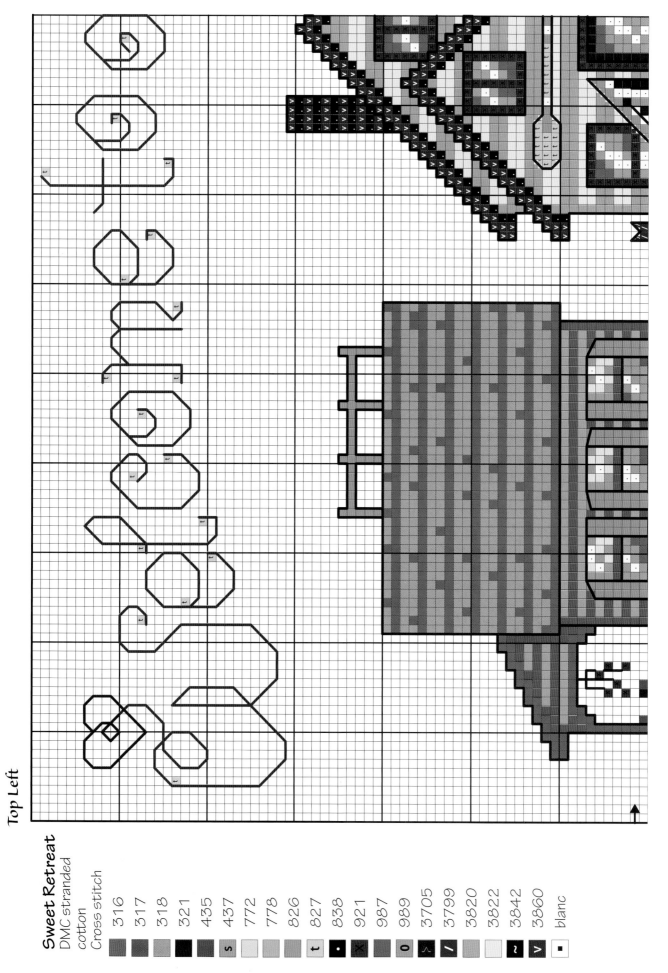

Sweet Retreat
DMC stranded
cotton
Cross stitch

	316
	317
	318
	321
	435
s	437
	772
	778
	826
t	827
•	838
✕	921
	987
0	989
∧	3705
/	3799
	3820
?	3822
v	3842
▪	3860
•	blanc

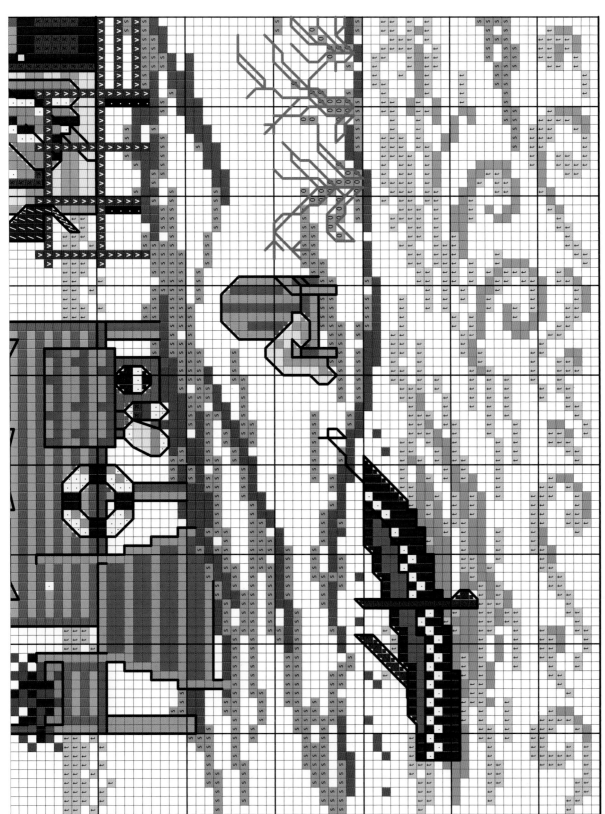

Backstitch
321
987
3799
3842
blanc

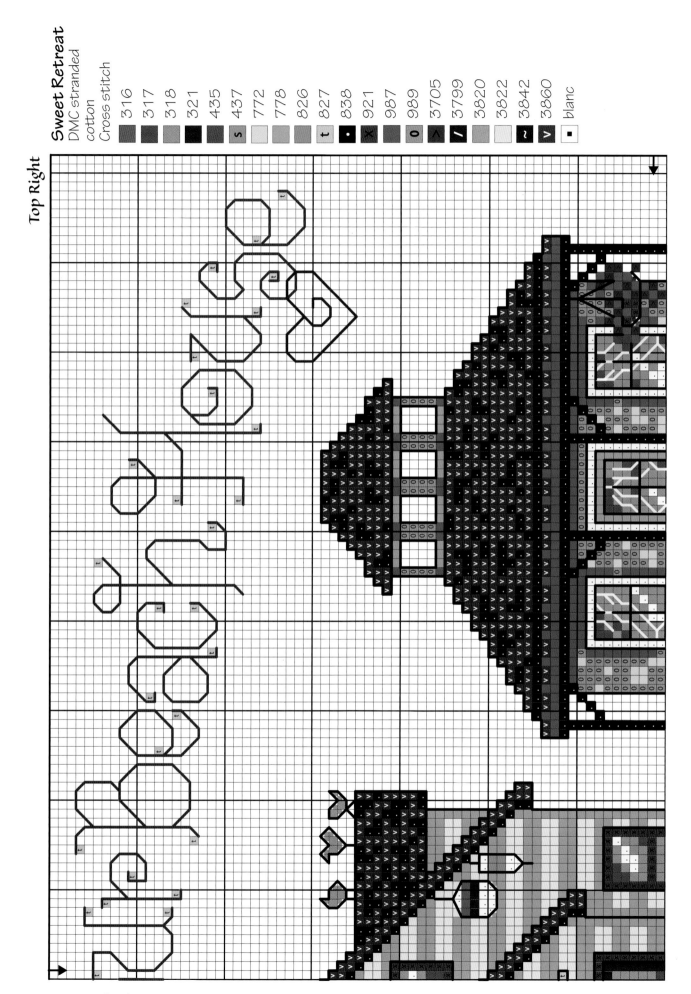

Backstitch
321
987
3799
3842
blanc

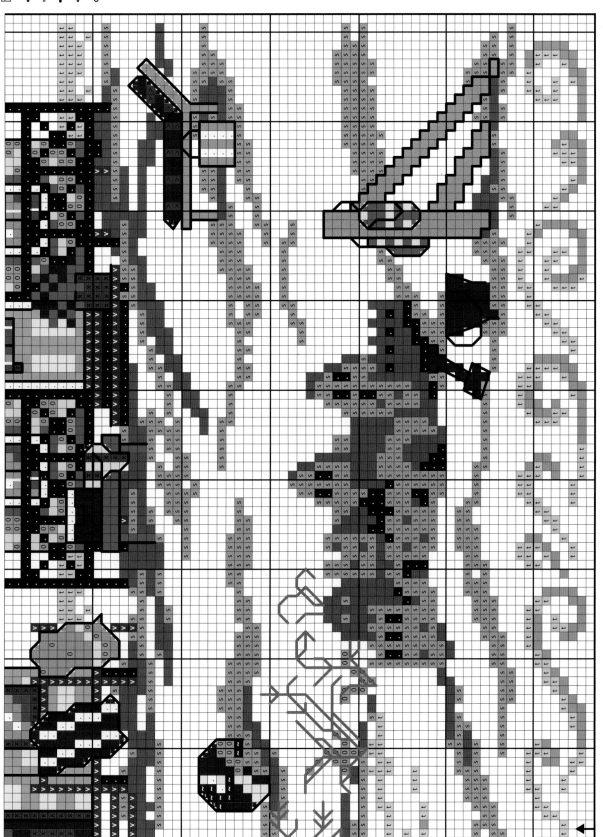

Cool Crustaceans

One of the pleasures of visiting a seaside town is eating local seafood. At the end of the day, fishermen may sell their catch from their boats or in a tiny, rustic seafood market. When you step into a fish market, delight in the fresh assortment of live lobsters and crabs in tanks, whole fish, clams and oysters. Choose your own catch of the day and bring it home to toast on the grill or boil in the pot. Simple recipes are always the best.

These bold lobster and crab pillows will remind you of these simple seaside pleasures and add the perfect touch to any seaside décor. If you prefer pastels or neutral colours, it's easy to change the thread or fabric colours to others of your choice. Alternatively, why not go wildly retro with zinging complementary colours? Try stitching the lobster in a golden amber on dark blue fabric and the crab in bright turquoise on orange fabric.

The clean, bold look of these two pillows is enhanced by working on white fabric. They would also make lovely framed pictures.

Lobster Pillow

This bright lobster design uses only whole cross stitch and a little backstitch in a single colour and makes a striking statement.

1 Prepare for work, referring to page 100 if necessary. Mark the centre of the fabric and centre of the chart overleaf. Mount your fabric in an embroidery frame if you wish.

2 Start stitching from the centre of the chart and fabric and work over two threads of evenweave. Use two strands of stranded cotton for cross stitches and one strand for backstitches. Once all stitching is complete, press the work.

Making up the pillow

3 Draw a pencil line 33 x 33cm (13 x 13in) around the stitched area, making sure the design is in the centre of the piece of evenweave.

4 Take the two pieces of backing fabric and fold one long edge back on each piece by 2.5cm (1in). Machine sew the seam flat (or use fusible webbing). Take your piping cord and tack (baste) it in place all around the marked area.

5 Place the two backing pieces on the front of the embroidery, overlapping the folded edges and the cord between the front and back (see Fig 1). Tack (baste) the layers together and then machine sew around the pillow using a 1.3cm (½in) seam. Trim the corners to reduce bulk and then turn through to the right side. Insert a cushion pad or refer to page 102 to make your own pillow form. Sew a large button to the back seam to secure.

Stitch count
100h x 77w

Design size
18.2 x 14cm (7⅛ x 5½in)

Finished size of pillow
33 x 33cm (13 x 13in)

You Will Need

White 20-count Lugana evenweave 40.6cm (16in) square (Zweigart code 3256/100/55)

Tapestry needle size 24–26

DMC stranded cotton (floss) as listed in the chart key

Backing fabric, two pieces each 35.5 x 25.5cm (14 x 10in)

Piping cord 183cm (72in) to tone

Cushion pad (or see page 102 to make your own)

Large button

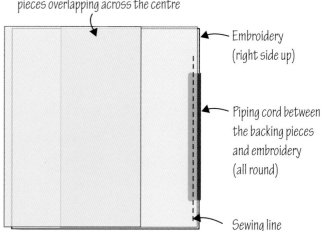

Two backing fabric pieces on top of the embroidery (right side down) with the pieces overlapping across the centre

Embroidery (right side up)

Piping cord between the backing pieces and embroidery (all round)

Sewing line

Fig 1
Making up the pillow cover

Crab Pillow

The crab design could be worked in a different shade, or you could experiment with a variegated thread to create a hand-shaded look, or be bold and use contemporary colour combinations.

1 Prepare for work, referring to page 100 if necessary. Mark the centre of the fabric and centre of the chart on page 21. Mount your fabric in an embroidery frame if you wish.

2 Start stitching from the centre of the chart and fabric and work over two threads of evenweave. Use two strands of stranded cotton for cross stitches and one strand for backstitches. Once all stitching is complete, press the work.

3 Make up the crab pillow in the same way as the lobster pillow, opposite. Note that the crab design in made up in a wide (landscape) format, rather than a tall (portrait) shape.

Stitch count
76h x 100w

Design size
14 x 18.2cm (5½ x 7⅛in)

Finished size of pillow
33 x 33cm (13 x 13in)

You Will Need

White 20-count Lugana evenweave (Zweigart code 3256/100/55) 40.6cm (16in) square

Tapestry needle size 24–26

DMC stranded cotton (floss) as listed in the chart key

Backing fabric, two pieces each 35.5 x 25.5cm (14 x 10in)

Piping cord 183cm (72in) to match thread colour

Cushion pad (or see page 102 to make your own)

Large button

'Live in the sunshine, swim in the sea, drink the wild air.' (Ralph Waldo Emerson)

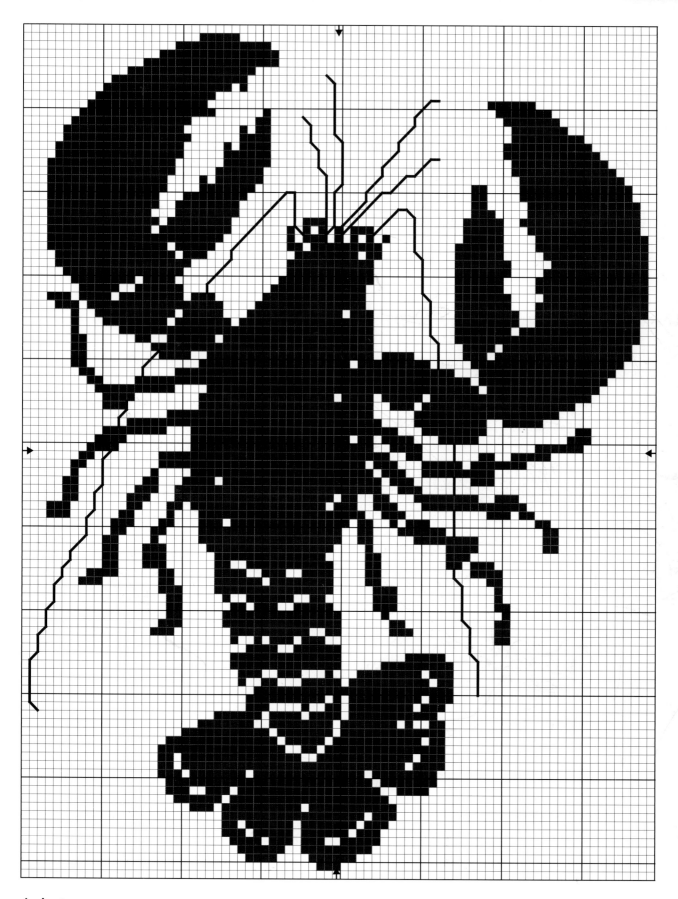

Lobster
DMC stranded cotton

Cross stitch   Backstitch

■ 321   —— 321

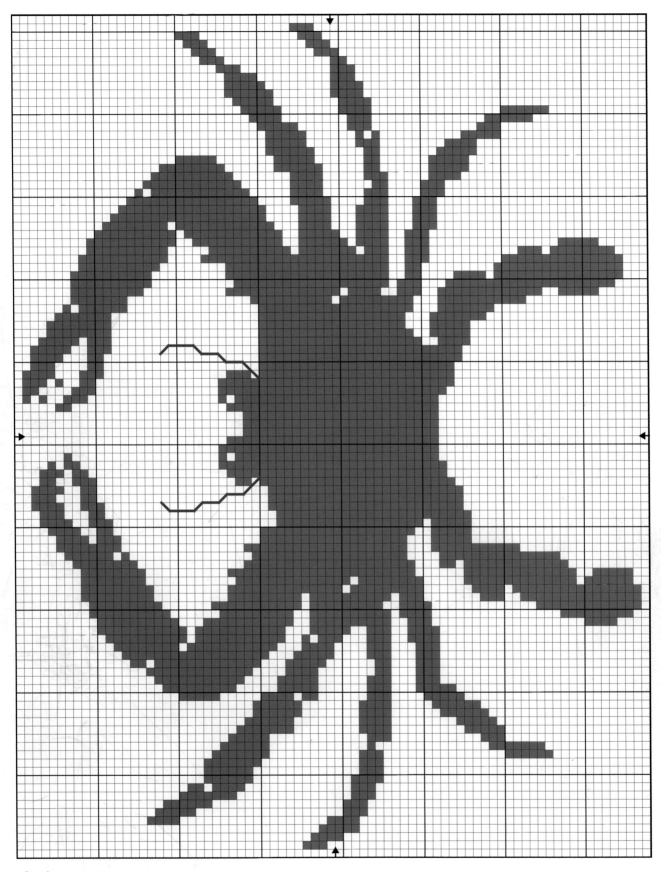

Crab
DMC stranded cotton

Cross stitch

Backstitch

▨ 3760

— 3760

Note: the chart has been rotated to fit the page but the design is made up as a wide not tall format

Tropical Party Time

Hang this evocative design of a tropical beach at sunset above your desk and escape to a foreign idyll as often as you want. The picture evokes dreams of a relaxed life, sipping cocktails and watching the sun sink over the sea. Little coloured crystals bring an extra sparkle to the design.

   Instead of just dreaming, this design may inspire you to throw your own beach party in your back garden and the other project ideas in this chapter will help your party go with a swing. Invite your girlfriends and serve drinks in fancy glasses as dance music toots in the background. Set the party table with a tropical print tablecloth and platters of fragrant food. Make some funky coasters to spark conversations about friends, jobs and exotic locations and some colourful bunting to flutter above coconut-scented candles. And a girlfriends' get together isn't complete without a hand-crafted purse to hold essentials. So, isn't it time to plan an evening with your friends to share secrets and small talk, to dream about faraway places and tropical sunsets?

This idyllic beach sunset picture is the inspiration behind the projects in this chapter and is sure to spark your creativity.

Beach Sunset Picture

Escape to a tropical island and add a touch of the tropics to your home with this lovely golden sunset picture. A few crystals scattered on the picture will give added sparkle to the design.

Stitch count
91h x 126w

Design size
16.5 x 23cm (6½ x 9in)

You Will Need

Yellow 14-count Aida
33 x 38cm (13 x 15in)

Tapestry needle size 24–26

DMC stranded cotton (floss)
as listed in the chart key

Heat-set crystals in assorted
colours (Kandi – see Suppliers)

Suitable picture frame

1 Prepare for work, referring to page 100 if necessary. Mark the centre of the fabric and centre of the chart on pages 34–35. Mount your fabric in an embroidery frame if you wish.

2 Start stitching from the centre of the chart and fabric and work over one Aida block. Use two strands of stranded cotton for full and three-quarter cross stitches and one strand for backstitches. Once all stitching is complete, press the work.

3 Add the crystals directly on to the stitched work (see page 102 for using heat-set crystals). I used them as a string of lights in the palm trees, on the hanging lanterns, for the sparkle on the water and on the cocktail glass.

4 Finish your picture by mounting and framing (see advice given on page 102).

'There is nothing more lovely than a wide stretch of sand, the ripple of blue waves and the delight of finding unexpected jewels from the sea wash up to your toes.'
(Ursula Michael)

Party Coasters

These inspirational party coasters are really easy to make and with the addition of some glitter are ideal for scattering on the table as the final glitzy touch to a tropical celebration.

Stitch count
(each design)
56h x 56w

Design size
(each design)
10.2 x 10.2cm (4 x 4in)

You Will Need

(each design)

14-count Aida (Bright Ideas, Charles Craft – see Suppliers) one 15.2cm (6in) square of Lemon Twist (#3976), Polar Ice (#5702) and Grasshopper (#4133)

Tapestry needle 24–26

DMC stranded cotton (floss) as listed in the chart key

Medium-weight iron-on interfacing, 11.5cm (4½in) square for each coaster

Craft glue with fine nozzle

Art glitter

1 Prepare for work, referring to page 100 if necessary. Mark the centre of the fabric and centre of the chart on page 32.

2 Start stitching from the centre of the chart and fabric and work over one Aida block. Use two strands of stranded cotton for cross stitches and two strands for backstitches. Once all stitching is complete, press the work.

3 Trim each embroidery to about 11.5cm (4½in) square. Take the squares of interfacing and fuse to the back of each embroidery (see page 102) and then trim to within three Aida blocks all round.

4 Add glitter swirls to the coasters by using a craft glue in a fine-nozzled container and squeezing the glue around the stitching in swirls and dots. Sprinkle the glue with glitter, shake off the excess and allow to dry.

Party Time Bunting

This no-sew bunting is a breeze to make; just stitch some tropical drink designs on colourful Aida, finish as a funky bunting and bring some real pizzazz to your next party.

1 Prepare for work, referring to page 100 if necessary. Mark the centre of each fabric square and the centre of the charted motifs on page 33. Use an embroidery frame if you wish.

2 Start stitching from the centre of the chart and fabric and work over one Aida block. Use two strands of stranded cotton for cross stitches and one strand for backstitches. Once all stitching is complete, press the work.

Making up the bunting

3 Trace the large flag template A from page 103 and use it to mark four triangles on your print fabric. You will need to allow sufficient space for each triangle to be flipped vertically (see Fig 1). Place the template on the first marked triangle and flip the template over vertically and mark a second triangle – this will create a diamond shape overall. Do this on the other three triangles. Cut out these four diamond shapes.

Stitch count
41h x 32w max

Design size
7.6 x 5.8cm (3 x 2¼in) max

Finished size of each flag
22.2 x 19cm (8¾ x 7½in)

You Will Need

14-count Aida (Bright Ideas, Charles Craft – see Suppliers), one 20.3cm (8in) square of Lemon Twist (#3976), Polar Ice (#5702) and Grasshopper (#4133)

Tapestry needle size 24–26

DMC stranded cotton (floss) as listed in the chart key

0.5m (½yd) tropical print fabric

0.5m (½yd) ultra-hold fusible adhesive

1m (1yd) black cord for stringing the bunting

Tracing paper and pencil

Fig 1

Create the flag using the large triangle template A from page 103. Mark the triangle once on your fabric, then flip the template over vertically and mark a second triangle to create a diamond shape. Cut out this shape

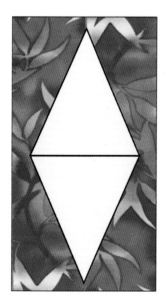

This colourful bunting will look great hanging from your drinks table and is sure to add fun and sparkle to any occasion. You can make the bunting longer by simply adding more flags.

4 Trace the small triangle template B from page 103 and use it to cut four pieces of fusible adhesive. On the first diamond, align the fusible adhesive on the wrong side of the print fabric in the position shown in Fig 2 and fuse into place. Remove the paper backing, fold the print fabric in half along the fold line shown on the diagram and fuse the two halves together. This will also create a casing at the top of the flag. Do the same with the other three diamonds.

5 Cut the large triangle template so it is about 2.5cm (1in) smaller all round (follow the dashed line on the template) and use this size to mark this smaller triangle on your four embroidered pieces. Back each embroidery with fusible adhesive and cut into the triangle shape. Peel the backing from the webbing, place each embroidery right side up and centrally on each of the flags and fuse in place. To make your bunting longer, add a fabric flag at each end or between the embroidered flags but do check you have sufficient fabric first.

6 When all the flags are assembled, thread the black cord through the channels at the top of each flag. To finish, add some heat-set crystals to the drink glasses and surrounding areas – see page 102.

Fig 2
Using the small triangle template B from page 103 cut a triangle of fusible adhesive. Fuse the adhesive to the lower part of the diamond shape

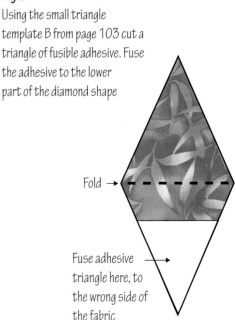

Fold →

Fuse adhesive triangle here, to the wrong side of the fabric

Tropical Bag

Make a splash at your next party with this colourful bag! Three flower designs have been provided so you can choose which one should adorn the flap of the bag – see also the suggestions in the box on page 30. The instructions given here are for a basic tote-style bag. The size of the bag, the flap and the tabs will need to be adjusted to fit your purchased handle. If you choose not to make a flap, you could secure the stitched work to the front of your bag with glue or double-sided, iron-on adhesive.

Stitch count
(for design shown)
48h x 37w

Design size
8.8 x 6.8cm (3½ x 2¾in)

Finished size of purse
21.5 x 20.3cm (8½ x 8in)
approx, excluding handles

You Will Need

14-count Aida 20.3cm (8in) square of Lemon Twist (Bright Ideas, Charles Craft #3976)

Tapestry needle 24–26

DMC stranded cotton (floss) as listed in the chart key

Tropical print fabric: two pieces each 50.8 x 30.5cm (20 x 12in) for the bag; one 30.5cm (12in) square for flap and four pieces 7.6 x 5cm (3 x 2in) for tabs

Lining fabric, two pieces each 50.8 x 30.5cm (20 x 12in)

Heavyweight fusible interfacing 30.5 x 50.8cm (12 x 20in)

Purchased handle

Beads and trims as desired

1 Prepare for work, referring to page 100 if necessary. Mark the centre of the fabric and centre of the charted flower motifs on page 31.

2 Start stitching from the centre of the chart and fabric and work over one Aida block. Use two strands of stranded cotton for cross stitches and one strand for backstitches. Once all stitching is complete, press the work.

Making up the bag

3 Begin by ironing the interfacing on to the back of the print fabric for the front of the bag (see page 102). Take the two 30.5 x 50.8cm (12 x 20in) pieces of print fabric and place them right sides together. Using 6mm (¼in) seams, sew the long side seams together (see Fig 1).

Fig 1
Sewing the two print fabric pieces, right sides together, along the long sides (dashed white lines) using 6mm (¼in) seams

← 30.5cm (12in) →

50.8cm (20in)

A funky handle and some colourful bead embellishments add a quirky finishing touch to this eyecatching bag.

4 Place your hands inside the bag and refold the bag so the side seams meet in the middle and on top of each other (see Fig 2). Measure 7.6cm (3in) up from the bottom left and bottom right corners and mark these points (see Fig 3). Draw a pencil line to join these marks. Sew across the marked lines and then trim off the corner triangles.

5 Using the two 30.5 x 50.8cm (12 x 20in) pieces of lining fabric, repeat the process above to make a lining bag. Turn the outside bag front side out and insert the lining into the bag. Fold back the top edges of the front and lining into the space between and topstitch to secure.

6 You will need to make four tabs. To make a tab, fold a 7.6 x 5cm (3 x 2in) piece of fabric in half lengthwise, right sides together. Sew a 6mm (¼in) seam down the length and across one short end. Trim the seam, turn right side out and press. Make three more tabs this way. Measure the space between your handles to gauge where to position the tabs. Sew the tabs to the top of the bag with a zigzag stitch, feed the tabs through the handles and sew the other ends of the tabs in place.

7 To make the flap, first measure the opening between the tabs. Cut two pieces of print fabric large enough to make a flap that will be sewn to the back edge of the bag and flipped over to the front. Be sure to measure your stitched work to fit on the front flap. Place the flap front and back fabrics right sides together and position the medium-weight interfacing on the back side. Sew around leaving a gap. Turn right side out through the gap and sew the opening closed.

8 Trim excess fabric around the embroidered flower to fit on the flap. Glue medium-weight interfacing to the back of the stitched work to stabilize the fabric. Glue or stitch the embroidery on the front flap. Glue decorative trim around the edges of the Aida as desired and allow to dry.

9 To make a beaded tassel, string several beads on strong thread and secure to the bottom of the front flap and on the handle if desired.

Fig 2
Re-folding the bag so the long side seams meet in the middle on top of each other

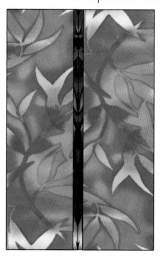

Fig 3
Creating a point to shape the bottom of the bag

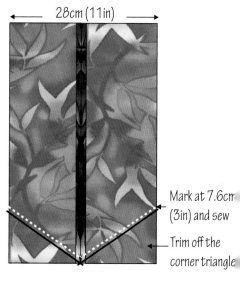

28cm (11in)

Mark at 7.6cm (3in) and sew

Trim off the corner triangle

Using the Flower Designs
The pink and mauve flowers are similar sizes and either can be used on the flap of the bag. If you want a larger design on the bag, or plan on making a larger bag, then the yellow flower could be used either on a larger flap or on the other side of the bag.

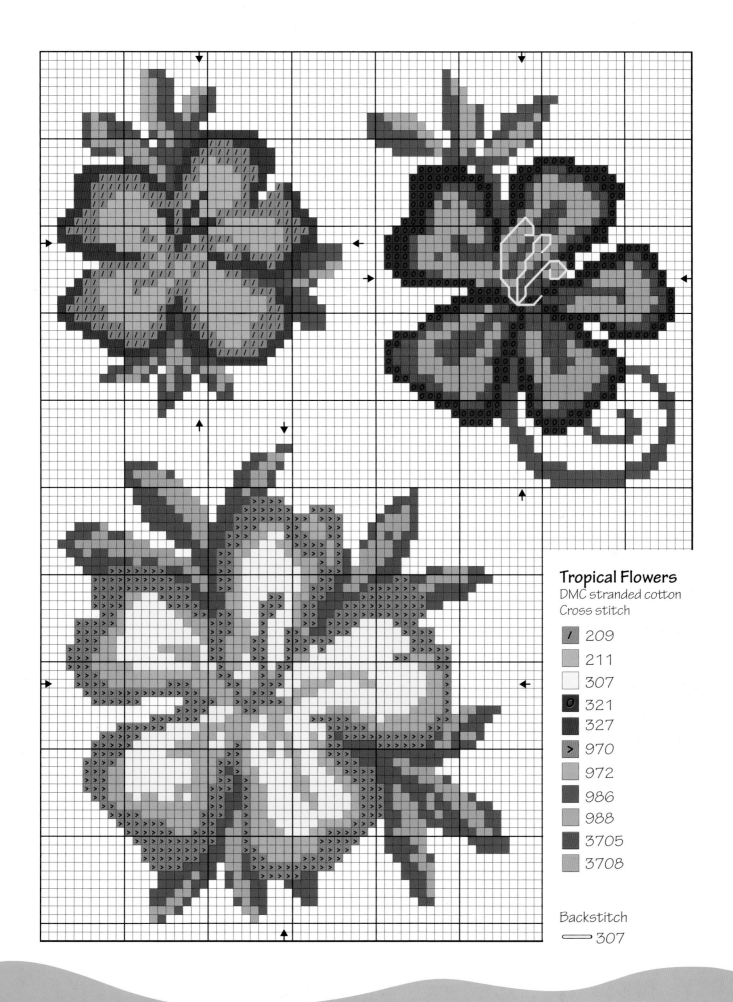

Tropical Flowers

DMC stranded cotton
Cross stitch

/	209
	211
	307
0	321
	327
>	970
	972
	986
	988
	3705
	3708

Backstitch

⎯ 307

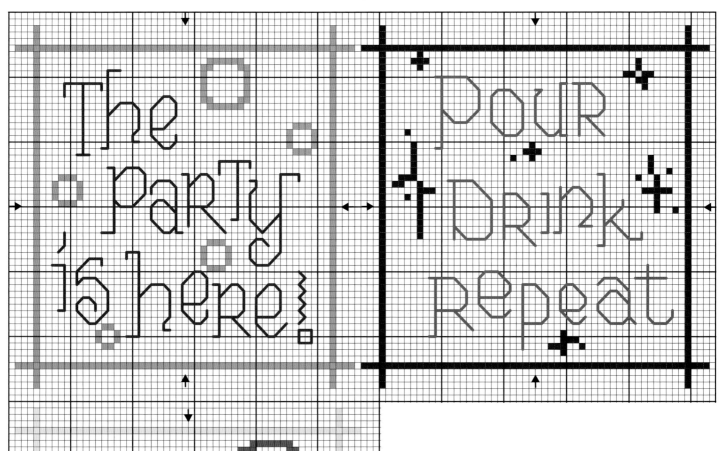

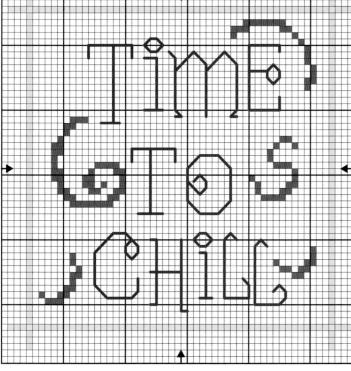

Party Coasters

DMC stranded cotton
Cross stitch

Backstitch

	307		3705
■	321		3845

—— 321
—— 327
—— 895

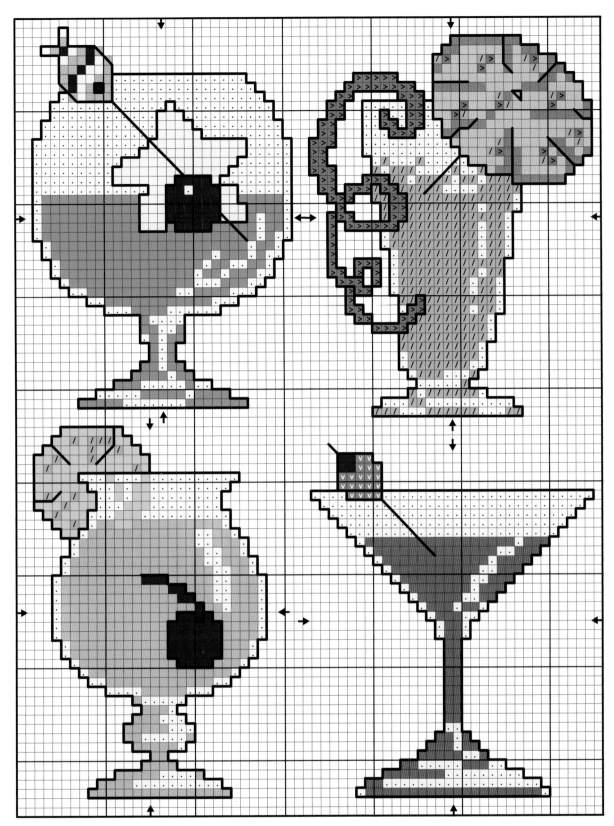

Party Time Bunting

DMC stranded cotton

Cross stitch

▨ 209	■ 321	> 970	■ 3031	• blanc
▨ 211	/ 906	972	3705	
307	907	V 988	3845	

Backstitch

— 3031

Beach Sunset

DMC stranded cotton

Cross stitch

L	154
O	470
■	666
>	742
–	816
▨	892
/	894
▨	907
☐	973
X	975
▨	976
▨	986
T	3021
▨	3032
V	3790
▨	3835
S	3836
▨	3838
▨	3840
·	blanc

Backstitch

——	816
——	986
——	3021

The Seashell Collection

A sandy stretch of beach is like an art canvas that is repainted every day with ocean treasures washed up by the tides. Every morning the beach is covered with a new landscape of seashells, sea glass, pebbles, driftwood and assorted weeds. These ribbons of treasure along the water's edge provide hours of entertainment for every collector. Who hasn't picked up a shell and reflected on the beauty of the unique colours? And don't we gather our friends in much the same way? Of the many people that pass us every day, only a few are selected, nurtured and tucked in our hearts. This charming sampler reminds us just how special these friends are – just like the shells, we can gaze at our friends and see that every one of them is different and special.

After you have stitched this lovely sampler, you could use individual shells to stitch on guest towels and make soap wraps and lotion bottle tags. You might find a weathered piece of wood to use as a base for a door hanger. When decorating a guest bedroom, a few shells stitched on personal items will let guests know that we treasure their friendship.

The sentiment on this lovely sampler makes it perfect to stitch and hang in your guest room, or just use some of the smaller motifs from the design for cards and gifts – see pages 40–42.

Friends Are Like Seashells Sampler

Your guests are sure to feel welcome when they see this pretty sampler in a room decorated with a serene beach theme. There are many small motifs within the design that could be used for quick-stitch projects.

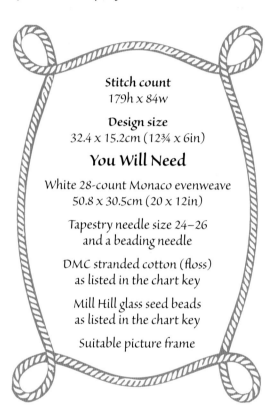

Stitch count
179h x 84w

Design size
32.4 x 15.2cm (12¾ x 6in)

You Will Need

White 28-count Monaco evenweave
50.8 x 30.5cm (20 x 12in)

Tapestry needle size 24–26
and a beading needle

DMC stranded cotton (floss)
as listed in the chart key

Mill Hill glass seed beads
as listed in the chart key

Suitable picture frame

1 Prepare for work, referring to page 100 if necessary. Mark the centre of the fabric and centre of the chart on pages 44–45. Mount your fabric in an embroidery frame if you wish.

2 Start stitching from the centre of the chart and fabric and work over two threads of evenweave. Use two strands of stranded cotton for full and three-quarter cross stitches and one strand for backstitches. Using matching thread and half cross stitch, attach the beads in the positions shown on the chart.

3 Once all stitching is complete, press the work and then finish your picture by mounting and framing (see page 102).

'Why do we love the sea? It is because it has some potent power to make us think things we like to think.'
(Robert Henri)

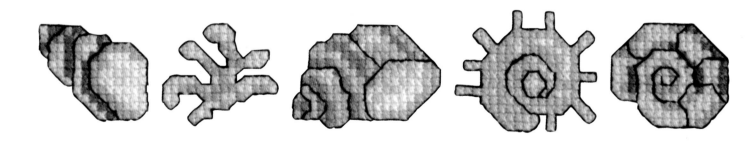

Guest Towel

After you have stitched the sampler you could select individual shells to stitch on guest towels – pick your favourites from the chart on pages 44–45. You could photocopy the chart and cut out the motifs required, sticking them on graph paper to arrange your own design.

1 Prepare for work and start stitching from the centre of the chart and fabric. Work over one Aida block, using two strands of thread for full and three-quarter cross stitches and one strand for backstitches.

2 Once stitching is complete, press. Sew on ribbons as desired, by hand or machine, above and below the stitched area.

Stitch count
(for design shown)
15h x 94w
Design size
2.5 x 17cm (1 x 6¾in)

You Will Need

Hand towel with Aida insert
(Charles Craft – see Suppliers)

Tapestry needle size 24–26

DMC stranded cotton (floss)
as listed in chart key

Assorted striped ribbons
the width of the towel

Stitch count
(for design shown)
12h x 14w
Design size
2.2 x 2.5cm (⅞ x 1in)

You Will Need

White 14-count Aida, at least 5cm (2in)
wide x length to wrap around your soap

Tapestry needle size 24–26

DMC stranded cotton (floss)
as listed in chart key

Bar of soap

Shell trim and narrow ribbon

Tacky glue

Soap Band

The simplest little idea can make guests feel special, such as wrapping a bar of scented soap in a length of embroidered Aida.

1 Prepare for work and start stitching from the centre of the charted motif and fabric. Work over one Aida block, using two strands of thread for full and three-quarter cross stitches and one strand for backstitches.

2 Once stitching is complete, press. Glue or sew the ends of the Aida together on the back of the soap to secure. Add shell trim and a ribbon bow to finish.

The main sampler is full of little motifs that can be used for gifts and keepsakes, such as the towel, soap band and lotion bottle tag shown here.

Ribbon Accents

The shells from the main sampler are perfect quick-stitch motifs to decorate lotion bottles, beauty products and cosmetic containers. All you need to do is choose and stitch your favourite shell and then make it up as a little patch and embellish as desired. See page 100 for calculating finished design sizes.

You Will Need

Scraps of white 14-count Aida about 10cm (4in) square

Tapestry needle size 24–26

DMC stranded cotton (floss) as listed in chart key

Scraps of fusible interfacing

Wide striped ribbon

Narrow ribbon to embellish

Glue or double-sided tape

1 Prepare for work and start stitching from the centre of the charted motif and centre of the fabric. Work over one Aida block, using two strands of thread for full and three-quarter cross stitches and one strand for backstitches.

2 Using a medium-hot iron, fuse interfacing to the back of the stitched area and then trim the stitched motif into a circle, or other shape as you desire. Use fabric glue or double-sided tape to fix the patch to a length of ribbon. Wrap around a bottle of lotion or other item and embellish with narrow ribbon as desired.

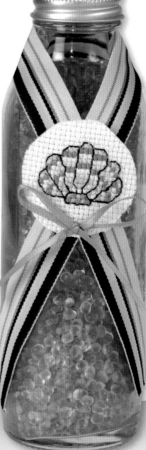

Gone to the Beach Hanger

When you are headed off to the beach for the afternoon, hang this little note on your doorknob to let everyone know where you are.

Stitch count
14h x 96w

Design size
2.5 x 18cm (1 x 7in)

You Will Need

White 14-count Aida
7.6 x 28cm (3 x 11in)

Tapestry needle size 24–26

DMC stranded cotton (floss)
as listed in the chart key

Piece of driftwood

Cording or pearl trim,
long enough for a hanger

Various shells, sea glass,
stones, beads and trim

Tacky glue

1 Prepare for work, referring to page 100 if necessary. Mark the centre of the fabric and the centre of the chart on page 45. Mount your fabric in an embroidery frame if you wish.

2 Start stitching from the centre of the chart and fabric and work over one Aida block. Use two strands of stranded cotton for the cross stitches. Use one strand to backstitch the shells and two strands for the wording. Once all stitching is complete, press the work.

3 Make up the hanger by first drilling two small holes at each end of the driftwood. Slip the cording into the holes and tie with a knot to secure. Trim the excess fabric around the stitched work into a free-form shape. Use tacky glue to fix the stitching to the driftwood. Glue assorted shells, glass, stones, beads and trim around the edges of the fabric and allow to dry.

Friends Are Like Seashells
DMC stranded cotton
Cross stitch

✓ 164	∧ 813	1 3743	V 3862
+ 543	− 826	✗ 3778	> 3864
598	989	3829	▢ ecru
676	3041	3830	• blanc
754	< 3371	▢ 3836	

Backstitch
— 826
— 989
— 3041
— 3371
— 3750

Mill Hill seed beads
◯ 00148 pale peach
◉ 03051 misty

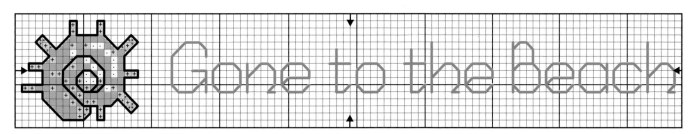

Gone to the Beach
DMC stranded cotton
Cross stitch

+ 543	754	• blanc

Backstitch
— 3371
— 826

Seaside Greetings

When I have the chance to get away to the shore for a few days, I like to bring along a stitching project. The needlework is not only a souvenir of my getaway but the therapy of stitching makes me slow down from my normal daily work schedule. One stitch at a time, one colour of thread at a time, allows my mind to settle into a rhythm like the constant lap of the ocean waves. This collection of small designs is ideal for stolen hours on summer afternoons whether you are at the beach or not.

The colours of summer are clear and bright. Many shades of blue reflect the endless sky and ocean. Red, orange and yellow are the warm, happy colours of beach umbrellas and flip-flops. This is the palette I've chosen for this collection of seaside greetings. These quick-to-stitch postcard designs are perfect to post to loved ones, or be mounted on a cork message board (see page 49) or finished as a photo album cover (see page 50).

The designs in this chapter are really easy to stitch and are perfect for decorating a wide range of items – see page 48 for suggestions. Stitching instructions for how to make up the journal shown here can be found on page 76.

Seaside Greetings Postcards

Like the varied, colourful prints on a beach blanket, each of these five postcard designs suggests an image seen at the shore on a summer's day.

1 Prepare for work, referring to page 100 if necessary. Mark the centre of the fabric and centre of the chart (pages 51–55). Mount your fabric in an embroidery frame if you wish.

2 Start stitching from the centre of the chart and fabric and work over one Aida block. Use two strands of stranded cotton for cross stitches and one strand for backstitches. Once all stitching is complete, press the work and trim the embroidery to the size you require.

Making up a postcard

3 Cut the interfacing and white backing fabric 2.5cm (1in) larger than the stitched area. With the embroidery face down, place the interfacing on top and then the backing and fuse together with a medium iron.

4 On the front of the work, draw a pencil line to within seven blocks of the stitched area. Using a zigzag stitch on a sewing machine, sew on the pencil line. (If you don't have a sewing machine you could work a blanket stitch all round instead.) Trim the fabric close to the zigzag stitching. Using a fabric marking pen, write a note on the back of the work. To mail your postcard, tuck it into an envelope and use proper postage.

Stitch count
60h x 80w (max)

Design size
10.8 x 14.5cm (4¼ x 5¾in) (max)

You Will Need
(for each postcard)

14-count Aida 25.5 x 28cm (10 x 11in)
(Charles Craft – see Suppliers):
Don't Miss the Boat – blush
(code CR-5463-1249-PK)
Wish You Were Here – Fiddler's Light
oatmeal (code FR-1903-5452-PK)
Gone to the Beach – blue
(code CR-5446-4600-PK)
Beach – Fiddler's Light oatmeal
(code FR-1903-5452-PK)
Fun in the Sun – yellow
(code CR-5444-7000-PK)

Tapestry needle size 24–26

DMC stranded cotton
(floss) as listed in the chart key

Medium-weight double-sided
fusible interfacing

White backing fabric
16.5 x 19cm (6½ x 7½in)

Fabric marking pen

There are other ways that you can use these postcard designs, such as mounting into a purchased message board and decorating with trims and bright buttons. You could also use the designs to adorn a beach bag or as patches sewn on to sun hats and T-shirts.

Photo Album

These designs are a good size for using with ready-made items, making it easy to create lovely gifts for friends and family. You can use a ready-made photo album or cover your own album, as described in steps 4–6 below.

1 Prepare for work, referring to page 100 if necessary. Mark the centre of the fabric and centre of the chart opposite. Mount your fabric in an embroidery frame if you wish.

2 Start stitching from the centre of the chart and fabric and work over one Aida block. Use two strands of stranded cotton for cross stitches and one strand for backstitches. Press the work and trim the embroidery to the size you require.

3 Glue the stitched work to the front of the album with tacky glue and then glue ric-rac over the raw edges of the Aida.

To cover your own album

4 Measure the length of the album and add 10cm (4in) to this measurement. Open the album and measure the total width of both covers and spine, and add 10cm (4in). Cut a piece of fabric to these sizes.

5 Place the fabric on a flat work surface, wrong side up. Place the album on the fabric and wrap 5cm (2in) of fabric over one inside cover and stick in place with double-sided tape or glue. Wrap the fabric around the book, placing tape or glue down the spine, and securing to the inside of the other cover in the same way.

6 Open the album and use scissors to snip where the book spine folds. Fold the top and bottom fabric over and secure with tape or glue. Tuck the spine fabric flap into the spine. To finish, stick a square of paper on the inside covers to hide the flaps of fabric.

Stitch count
58h x 77w

Design size
10.5 x 14cm (4⅛ x 5½in)

You Will Need

Yellow 14-count Aida 25.5 x 28cm (10 x 11in) (Charles Craft code CR-5444-7000-PK)

Tapestry needle size 24–26

DMC stranded cotton (floss) as listed in the chart key

Photo album, approx 19 x 23cm (7½ x 9in) – from stationers

Ric-rac trim 66cm (26in) long

Tacky glue or double-sided tape

Fun in the Sun
DMC stranded cotton
Cross stitch

321 797 798 906 947 964 3705 3851 blanc

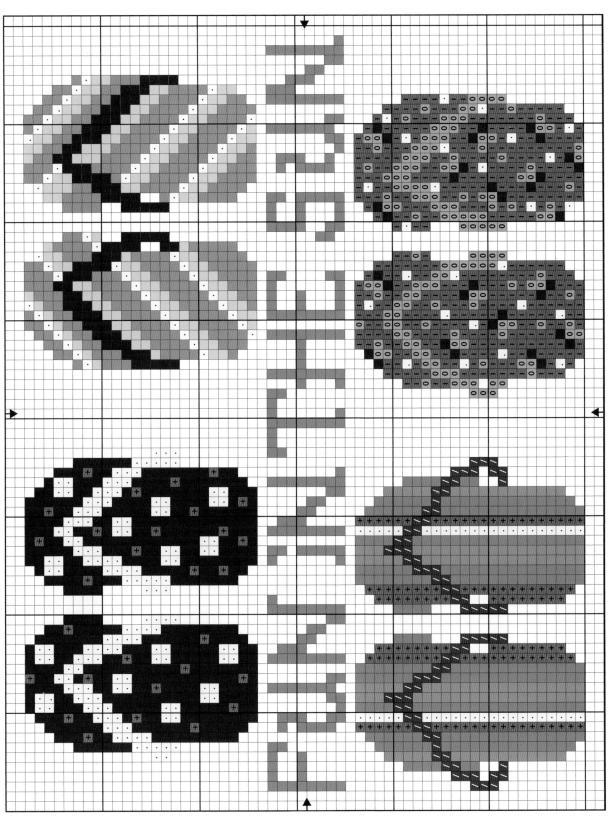

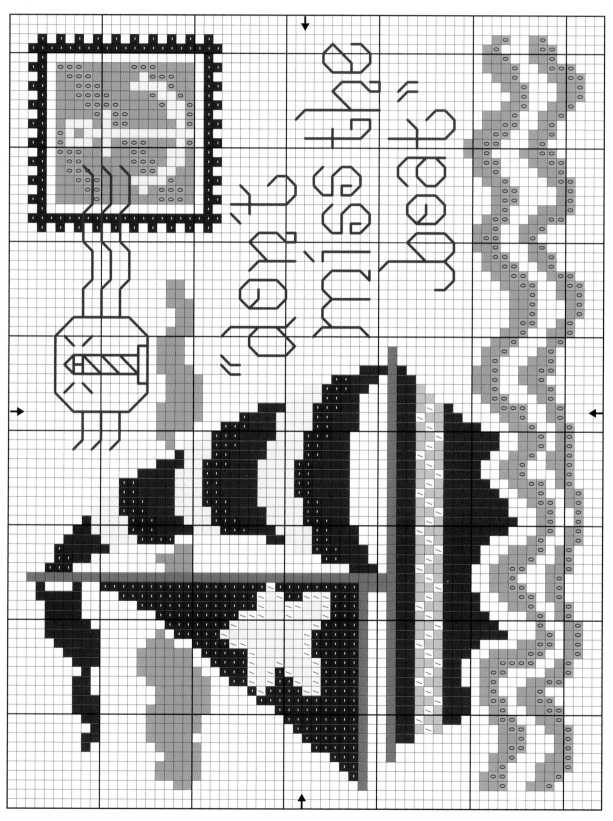

Don't Miss the Boat

DMC stranded cotton
Cross stitch

- 307
- 321
- 680
- 797
- 972
- 996
- 3851
- blanc

Backstitch
— 797

Gone to the Beach
DMC stranded cotton
Cross stitch

	307
●	310
＞	797
	798
	906
	947
	964
	972
—	996
	3851
✓	blanc

Backstitch
—— 797
—— blanc

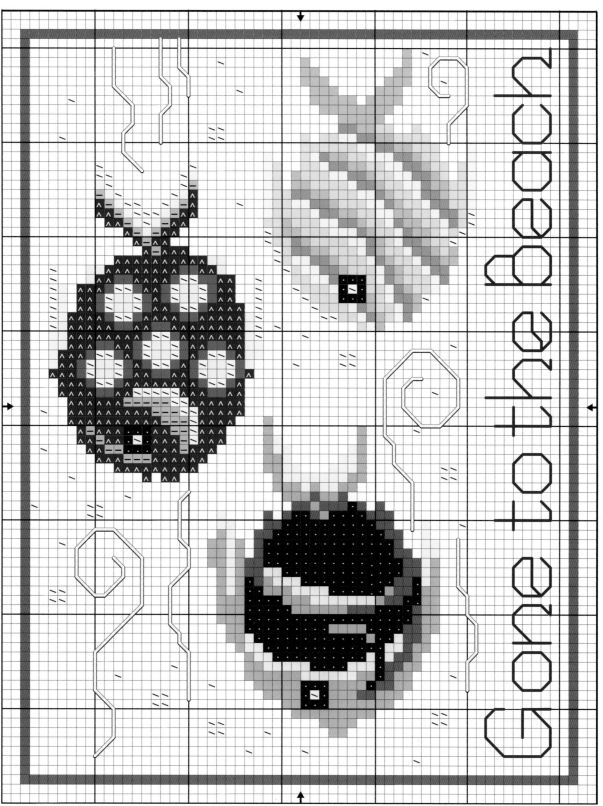

307
321
414
680
798
906
947
964
996

Backstitch
— 310

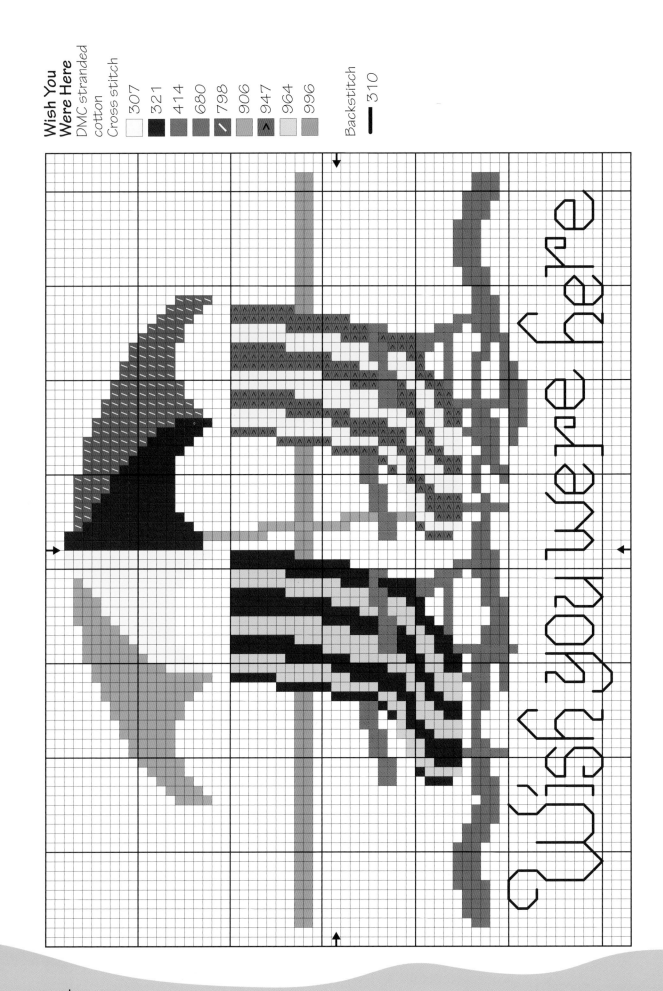

307
310
321
680
797
798
906
947
964
3705
3851

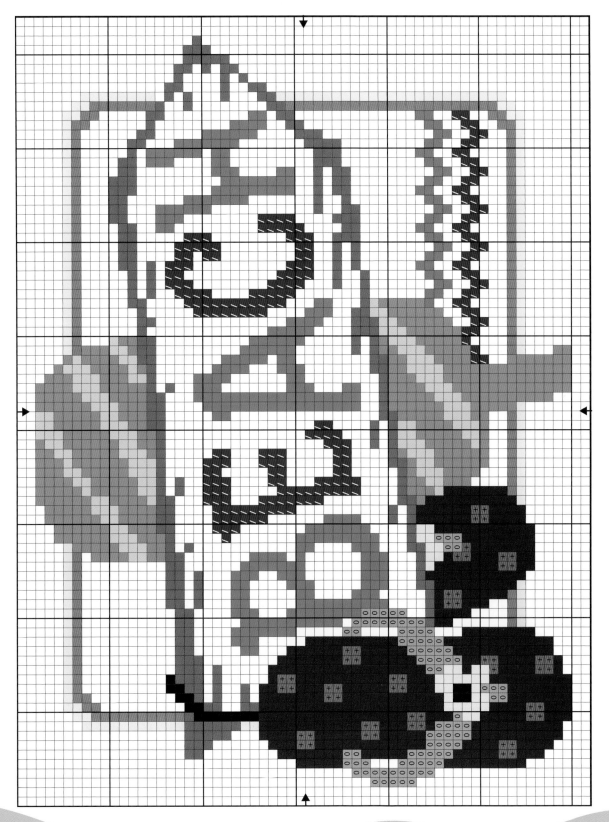

Call of the Sea Birds

One of the pleasures of spending time by the water is watching the birds in their native habitat as they feed, nest and sing. I have chosen four of my favourites to create this elegant set of framed pictures to remind you of the natural beauty of the coast all around you.

Catching a glimpse of the tall white ibis wading in coastal swamps makes me think of a graceful ballerina slowly moving to a soft lullaby. The sandpipers are a family of birds that scoot back and forth between the waves, probing the sand with their long bills as they search for invertebrates. Looking like little boys in formal attire, chubby puffins waddle and breed on rocky shorelines in the cold northern seas during the summer and overwinter in the open ocean as they search for small fish. Pelicans are large, fish-eating water birds. Their expandable throat pouches are used rather like fishing nets as they sweep their beaks along the surface waters. You may not see these four species together in a single marine environment but they certainly make a most handsome collection for us to admire in our homes.

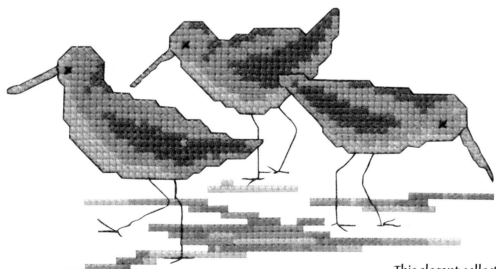

This elegant collection of sea birds will make a lovely statement in a more formal room. The delicate pearl grey linen provides just the right hazy background, while the backstitched birds' names pull the four pictures together as a set.

Sea Birds Pictures

Studying the behaviour and characteristics of birds is a fascinating pastime, particularly if the results are some charming portraits. The designs have been worked over two threads of a linen fabric but you could also stitch them over one block of 14-count Aida.

Stitch count
(each design)
84h x 84w

Design size
15.2 x 15.2cm (6 x 6in)

You Will Need
(for each design)

Pearl grey 28-count Cashel linen (Zweigart code #3821/705/55) 30.5cm (12in) square

Tapestry needle size 24–26

DMC stranded cotton (floss) as listed in the chart key

Suitable picture frame, 20.3cm (8in) square

1 Prepare for work, referring to page 100 if necessary. Mark the centre of the fabric and centre of the chart (pages 60–63). Mount your fabric in an embroidery frame if you wish.

2 Start stitching from the centre of the chart and fabric and work over two threads of the linen. Use two strands of stranded cotton for full and three-quarter cross stitches and one strand for backstitches.

3 Once stitching is complete, press the work and then frame as desired (see page 102). Simple wooden frames were used in these models.

'For all at last return to the sea – to Oceanus, the ocean river, like the ever-flowing river of time, the beginning and the end.'
(Rachel Carson)

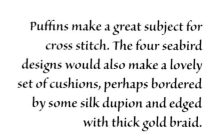

Puffins make a great subject for cross stitch. The four seabird designs would also make a lovely set of cushions, perhaps bordered by some silk dupion and edged with thick gold braid.

White Ibis
DMC stranded cotton
Cross stitch

Backstitch

0 415	798	977
469	809	3031
471	970	✓ blanc

Backstitch
— 977
— 3031

Sandpipers
DMC stranded cotton
Cross stitch

Backstitch

	162	0	543	■	3031		3864	— 3031
	437	-	813	■	3777			— 3862
	523		826	V	3862			

Puffins

DMC stranded cotton
Cross stitch

■ 310	0 415	■ 796	■ 970
✗ 318	■ 646	^ 798	∕ blanc
V 350	■ 648	■ 809	

Backstitch

— 310

— 350

Pelican
DMC stranded cotton
Cross stitch

Backstitch

■ 301	⊙ 721	■ 792	T 3839
■ 414	■ 722	■ 801	3840
+ 437	V 739	- 3031	⁄ blanc

Backstitch
— 301
— 437
— 3031

Sail Away

Sailing is more a state of mind than reaching any destination. The breeze that moves you away from the busy city serenely across the smooth water, clears the thoughts from your head in a matter of minutes. Sails, pure white or as colourful as any rainbow, flutter above you, while the flying spray splashes your face. For all those non-sailors among you, who prefer to be on shore looking at yachts scudding across the water, there are some wonderful projects in this chapter for you to enjoy.

There is a captivating assortment of sailboats housed within a sturdy tray (shown opposite), which could also be framed as a picture. A handy magazine holder (see page 69), made up in a style that might be found inside a sailing ship, will keep your books tidy and makes a great gift. And what fun it would be to carry the beach tote shown below on summer errands, personalized with a sailboat motif.

The four sailboat designs in this chapter fit perfectly into this useful tray but the designs could be used in many other ways, perhaps as a set of small framed pictures or as greetings cards.

Tray

Use this tray as an attractive serving piece all year long. As an alternative finish, this design would look lovely in a crisp picture frame with a mount (mat) that picks up a colour from the embroidery.

Stitch count
118h x 118w

Design size
21.5 x 21.5cm (8½ x 8½in)

You Will Need

White 14-count Aida
40.6cm (16in) square

Tapestry needle size 24–26

DMC stranded cotton (floss)
as listed in the chart key

Tray for needlework 25.5cm (10in)
square (Sudberry House
– see Suppliers)

1 Prepare for work, referring to page 100 if necessary. Mark the centre of the fabric and centre of the chart (pages 70–71). Mount your fabric in an embroidery frame if you wish.

2 Start stitching from the centre of the chart and fabric and work over one block of Aida. Use two strands of stranded cotton for full and three-quarter cross stitches and one strand for backstitches.

3 Once stitching is complete, press the work and mount in the tray following the manufacturer's instructions.

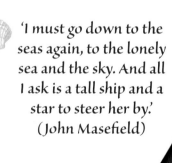

'I must go down to the seas again, to the lonely sea and the sky. And all I ask is a tall ship and a star to steer her by.'
(John Masefield)

Purse

When going shopping or to the beach, a summery purse or tote bag is a must. An easy way to decorate a pre-made bag is to stitch any of the sailboats, make it into a patch and glue it on the front of the bag.

Stitch count
(for design shown)
47h x 49w

Design size
12 x 12.5cm (4¾ x 5in)

You Will Need

White 20-count Lugana evenweave
25.5cm (10in) square

Tapestry needle size 24–26

DMC stranded cotton (floss)
as listed in the chart key

Fusible fleece

Decorative braid 61cm (24in)

Ribbon bow

Purchased purse or bag

Tacky glue

1 Prepare for work, referring to page 100 if necessary. Mark the centre of the fabric and centre of the motif (pages 70–71). Mount your fabric in an embroidery frame if you wish.

2 Start stitching from the centre of the motif and fabric and work over two threads of evenweave. Use three strands of stranded cotton for full and three-quarter cross stitches and one strand for backstitches. Once complete, press the work.

3 To make the design into a patch, draw a pencil line about 2.5cm (1in) away from the stitched area on the front side. Fuse the fleece to the back of the stitched work covering the pencil line. Trim on the pencil line to remove excess fabric.

4 Apply glue to the back of the work and press into position on the purse, making sure no glue oozes out at the sides. Glue on the braid to cover the raw edges of the embroidery all round and finish by gluing on a ribbon bow to cover the raw ends of the braid.

Magazine Holder

Select three of the sailboat motifs to create a handy magazine holder. Ric-rac trim, natural rope and nautical-style buttons add unique finishing touches.

1 Prepare for work, referring to page 100 if necessary. Mark the centres of the pieces of Aida and centre of the charted motifs (pages 70–71).

2 Start stitching from the centre of the motif and fabric and work over one block of Aida. Use two strands of stranded cotton for full and three-quarter cross stitches and one strand for backstitches. Once stitching is complete, press the squares.

Making up the magazine holder

3 To make the front panel of the magazine holder, layer an outer fabric piece with a lining fabric piece, right sides together and then place the interfacing on the lining. With a pencil, draw the point on the interfacing at the bottom end. Sew the side seams and the point at the bottom end, leaving the top open. Trim excess fabric and turn the panel right side out. Tuck in the raw edges at the top, tack (baste) the gap closed and press the work. Make a back panel in the same way.

4 Trim each of the stitched pieces to 12.7cm (5in) square. Position the squares on the front panel as in Fig 1 opposite and glue in place. Glue the ric-rac around the Aida squares to hide the raw edges and allow the glue to dry.

5 Place the front panel on the back panel matching the linings. With pins, mark the sewing lines as shown in Fig 1. Topstitch the edges of the panels, leaving the side openings unstitched. Topstitch horizontally between the Aida squares.

 'Never a ship sails out of the bay but carries my heart away.'
(Roselle Mercier Montgomery)

Stitch count
(each design)
49h x 52w

Design size
9 x 9.4cm (3½ x 3¾in)

Finished size of holder
16.5 x 66cm (6½ x 26in)
excluding hanger

You Will Need

White 14-count Aida, three 23cm (9in) squares

Tapestry needle size 24–26

DMC stranded cotton (floss) as listed in the chart key

Two pieces of outer fabric for the holder each 71 x 18cm (28 x 7in)

Two pieces of lining fabric each 71 x 18cm (28 x 7in)

Two pieces of medium-weight fusible interfacing each 71 x 18cm (28 x 7in)

Blue ric-rac trim 190cm (72in) long

White rope trim 1.3cm (½in) thick x 152cm (60in) long

Thick dowel or purchased hanger 1.3cm (½in) x 20.5cm (8in) long

Six nautical-style buttons

Permanent fabric adhesive

Fig 1

Gluing the embroidered Aida squares into position and then marking the sewing lines.

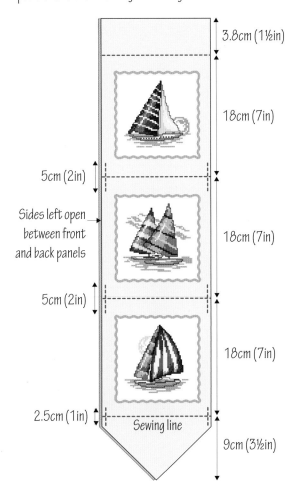

3.8cm (1½in)

18cm (7in)

5cm (2in)

Sides left open between front and back panels

18cm (7in)

5cm (2in)

18cm (7in)

2.5cm (1in)

Sewing line

9cm (3½in)

6 Sew a button on to the top left and bottom right corners of the Aida squares. Cut the rope trim into five equal pieces. Tie a knot at each end of four of the ropes. Glue the knotted rope trim on the fabric between the Aida squares.

7 Insert the dowel into the top sleeve opening. To finish, make a hanger with the remaining rope, gluing it to each end of the dowel.

This useful holder shows off the sailboat designs beautifully. It can house magazines or books, or simply be used as a jaunty wall hanging.

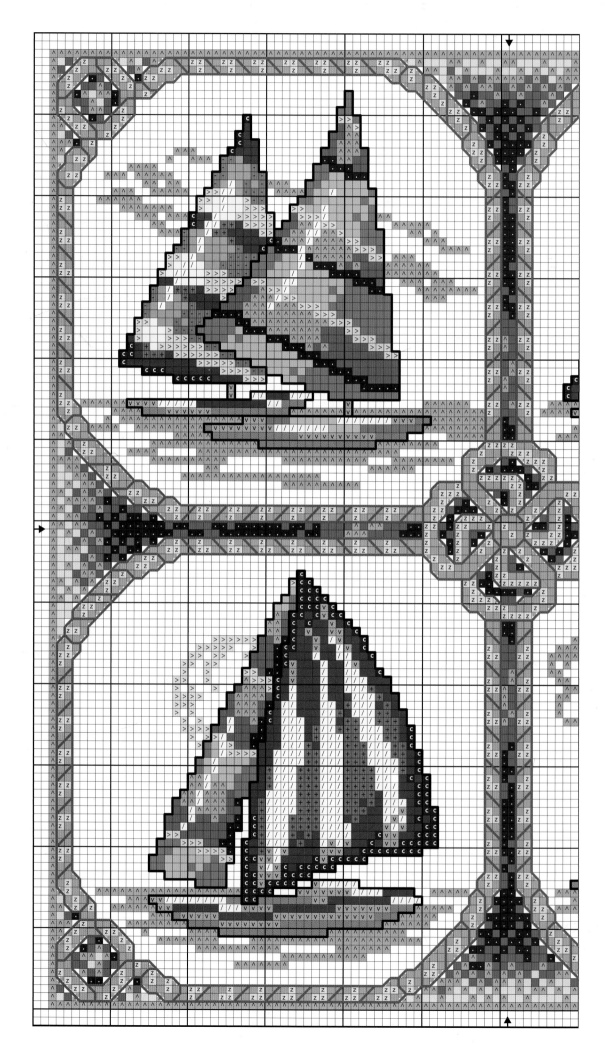

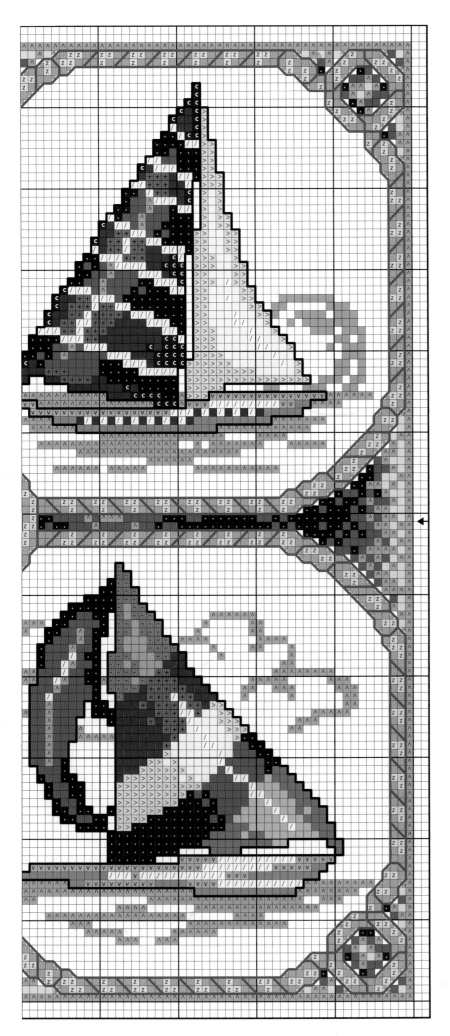

Sail Away
DMC stranded cotton
Cross stitch

▨	162	▨	740
▨	318	∧	813
▨	349	C	816
+	351	▪	825
V	415	▨	826
▨	422	▨	905
Z	677	▨	907
>	725	-	947
▨	727	/	blanc

Backstitch
— 310
— 869

Sea Life Friends

Have you ever watched a child build a sandcastle? With a shovel and bucket, they concentrate on creating a masterpiece. And after the project is complete, they may jump in the water and ride the waves over and over again. After a bite to eat, they are off again collecting seashells or tossing a ball on the sand. When my children were small, I spent many relaxing hours stitching my projects as they played. At the end of the day, they were exhausted and would nod off on the trip home.

This chapter features a collection of fun sea life friends perfect for children – decorative motifs that will remind them of days at the beach long after school has started again. Quick to stitch and finish, these designs can be made in just a few hours. Refer to the charts for the stitch counts. Ideas have been given for using the designs but there are lots of other ways they could be displayed – just become a child again and use your imagination!

In this chapter there are 12 cheerful motifs (charted on pages 78–81) and most of the designs have been finished as patches, which can be sewn or glued to almost anything. Both the shrimp design shown right and the starfish shown left would be easy first projects as they have been stitched on to ready-made items with an Aida insert (see Suppliers).

Beach Cover-Up

A girl's beach cover-up takes on additional charm with a pretty seahorse patch (see picture on previous page). The patch could also be used to decorate a beach hat.

Stitch count
49h x 24w

Design size
9 x 4.4cm (3½ x 1¾in)

You Will Need

Pale pink 28-count Cashel linen 15cm (6in) square (Zweigart code 3821/4034/55)

Tapestry needle size 24–26

DMC stranded cotton (floss) as listed in the chart key

Medium-weight fusible interfacing

Narrow ric-rac trim 46cm (18in) long

Purchased beach cover-up

1 Prepare for work, referring to page 100 if necessary. Mark the centre of the fabric and centre of the charted motif.

2 Start stitching from the centre of the chart and fabric and work over two threads of linen. (If preferred, you could stitch over one block of a 14-count Aida.) Use two strands of stranded cotton for full and three-quarter cross stitches and one strand for backstitches. Once stitching is complete, press the work.

3 Trace an oval slightly larger than the stitched area on the interfacing. Centre the interfacing on the back of the stitching and fuse. Trim excess fabric on the oval line. Tack (baste) the patch to the garment and then hand sew the ric-rac in place to cover the raw edges of the patch.

You will have fun choosing garments and objects to decorate with the designs in this chapter. For example, the crab could be used on a sun hat, the dolphin on a boy's cover-up and the turtle on a sun visor. See the charts for the stitch counts and page 100 for calculating finished design sizes.

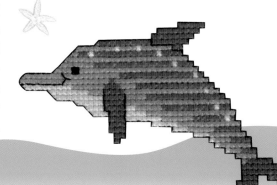

Beach Bag

Every little girl dreams of mermaids swimming in the deep oceans. Stitch up a cheerful mermaid on a ready-made bag, bring it along to the beach and watch her smile light up. The bag is shown on page 73.

Stitch count
49h x 78w

Design size
9 x 14.2cm (3½ x 5½in)

You Will Need

14-count Aida ready-made bag in grasshopper green (Charles Craft Bright Ideas – see Suppliers)

Tapestry needle size 24–26

DMC stranded cotton (floss) as listed in the chart key

Heat-set crystals

Wide ric-rac trim 23cm (9in) long

Two ribbon bows

Permanent fabric glue

1 Prepare for work, referring to page 100 if necessary. Mark the centre of the front fabric on the bag and the centre of the charted motif on page 78.

2 Start stitching from the centre of the chart and fabric and work over one block of Aida. Use two strands of stranded cotton for full and three-quarter cross stitches and one strand for backstitches. Once stitching is complete, press the work.

3 Apply the heat-set crystals around the stitched area (see page 102). To finish, glue the ric-rac and bows to the bag using the picture on page 73 as a guide.

'Was there ever a child set free to choose that didn't settle for a day by the sea?'
(Ursula Michael)

Journal

Memories of a beach holiday penned in a journal decorated with a fun octopus will be cherished many years from now.

Stitch count
45h x 54w

Design size
8.2 x 10cm (3¼ x 4in)

You Will Need

Grasshopper green 14-count Aida 15cm (6in) square (Charles Craft Bright Ideas – see Suppliers)

Tapestry needle size 24–26

DMC stranded cotton (floss) as listed in the chart key

Fusible fleece

Journal or photo album

Decorative paper to cover the front of the journal

Beach-themed stickers

Permanent fabric glue

1 Prepare for work, referring to page 100 if necessary. Mark the centre of the fabric and centre of the charted motif. Mount your fabric in an embroidery frame if you wish.

2 Start stitching from the centre of the chart and fabric and work over one block of Aida. Use two strands of stranded cotton for full and three-quarter cross stitches and one strand for backstitches. Once stitching is complete, press the work.

3 Draw an oval slightly larger than the stitched area on the fusible fleece. Fuse the fleece to the back of the work (see page 102) and trim excess fabric on the oval line.

4 Trim decorative paper to fit the journal cover and glue in place. Glue the stitched work to the cover and then decorate the cover with stickers.

Gift Box

This silly little stingray was made up as a patch and glued to the top of a purchased box – great for holding seaside treasures.

Stitch count
43h x 47w

Design size
7.6 x 8.5cm (3 x 3⅜in)

You Will Need

Lemon twist 14-count Aida 15cm (6in) square (Charles Craft Bright Ideas – see Suppliers)

Tapestry needle size 24–26

DMC stranded cotton (floss) as listed in the chart key

Fusible fleece

Purchased box

Embellishments as desired

Permanent fabric glue

1 Prepare for work, referring to page 100 if necessary. Mark the centre of the fabric and centre of the charted motif.

2 Start stitching from the centre of the chart and fabric and work over one block of Aida. Use two strands of stranded cotton for full and three-quarter cross stitches and one strand for backstitches. Once stitching is complete, press the work.

3 On the fusible fleece, draw a square slightly larger than the stitched area. Fuse the fleece to the back of the work and then trim excess fabric on the square line.

4 Glue the work to the box top and decorate the rest of the box as desired.

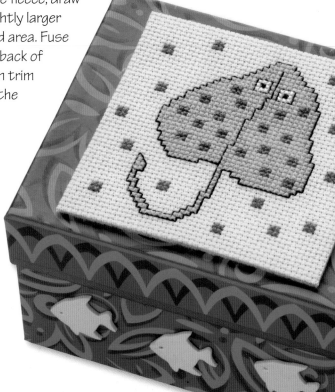

 These colourful fish would be ideal to decorate a coat rack or a pencil box – perfect for storing pens and pencils to record seaside holiday events in a journal. See the charts on page 79 for the stitch counts.

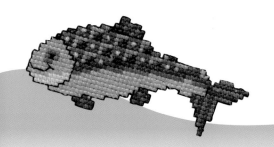

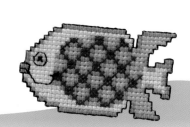

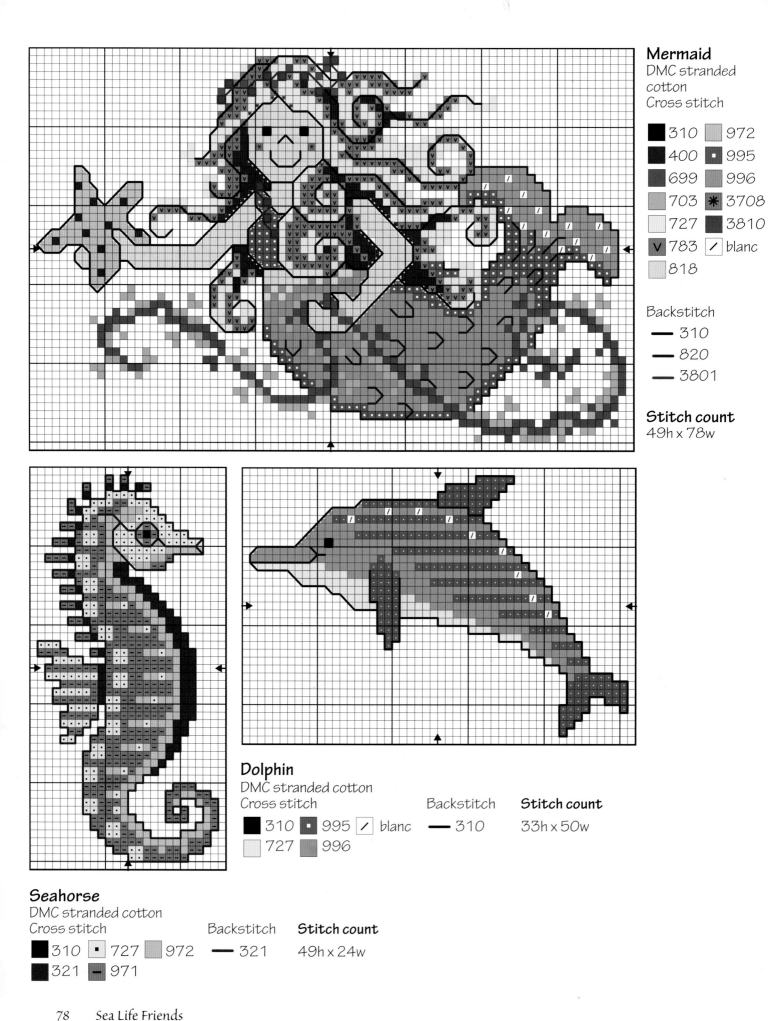

Mermaid
DMC stranded cotton
Cross stitch

- ■ 310
- ■ 400
- ■ 699
- □ 703
- □ 727
- ⩔ 783
- □ 818
- ▨ 972
- ▣ 995
- ▨ 996
- ✳ 3708
- ■ 3810
- ╱ blanc

Backstitch
- — 310
- — 820
- — 3801

Stitch count
49h x 78w

Dolphin
DMC stranded cotton
Cross stitch

- ■ 310
- □ 727
- ▣ 995
- ▨ 996
- ╱ blanc

Backstitch
- — 310

Stitch count
33h x 50w

Seahorse
DMC stranded cotton
Cross stitch

- ■ 310
- □ 321
- ▪ 727
- ▨ 971
- ▨ 972

Backstitch
- — 321

Stitch count
49h x 24w

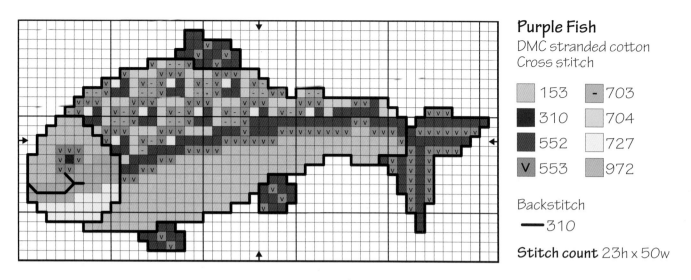

Purple Fish
DMC stranded cotton
Cross stitch

153		-	703
■	310		704
■	552		727
V	553		972

Backstitch
— 310

Stitch count 23h x 50w

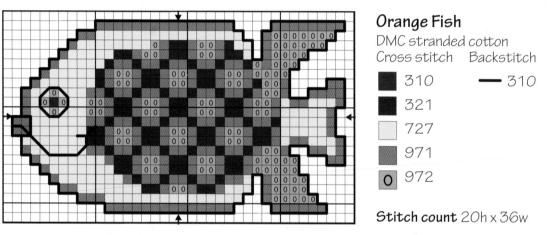

Orange Fish
DMC stranded cotton

Cross stitch   Backstitch

■ 310		— 310
■ 321		
727		
971		
O 972		

Stitch count 20h x 36w

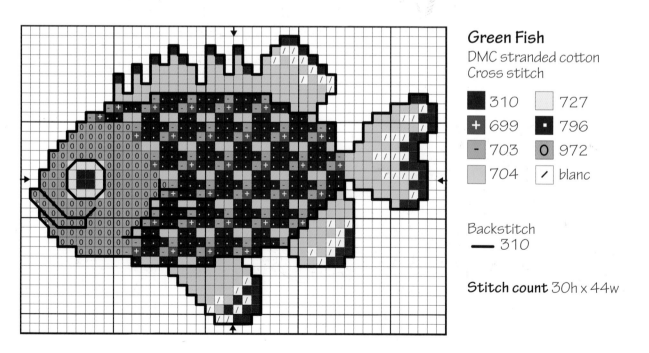

Green Fish
DMC stranded cotton
Cross stitch

■	310		727
+	699	■	796
-	703	O	972
	704	/	blanc

Backstitch
— 310

Stitch count 30h x 44w

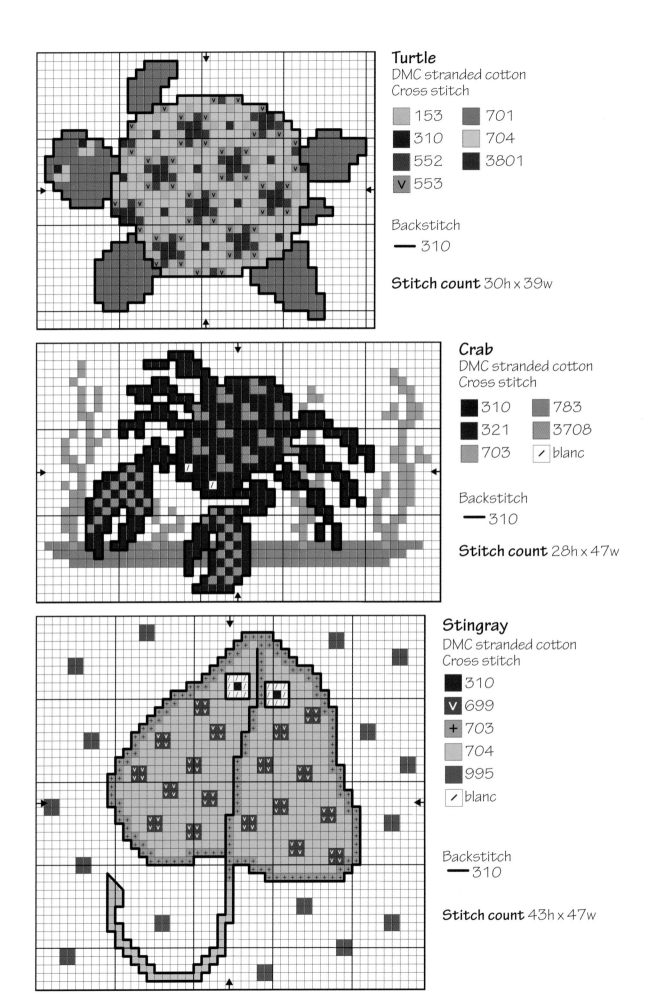

Turtle
DMC stranded cotton
Cross stitch

- 153
- 310
- 552
- V 553
- 701
- 704
- 3801

Backstitch
— 310

Stitch count 30h x 39w

Crab
DMC stranded cotton
Cross stitch

- 310
- 321
- 703
- 783
- 3708
- / blanc

Backstitch
— 310

Stitch count 28h x 47w

Stingray
DMC stranded cotton
Cross stitch

- 310
- V 699
- + 703
- 704
- 995
- / blanc

Backstitch
— 310

Stitch count 43h x 47w

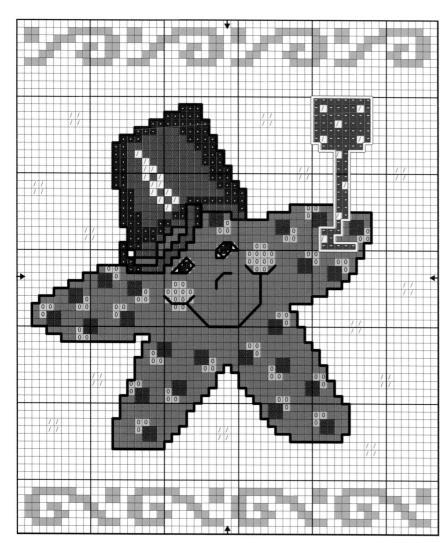

Starfish
DMC stranded cotton

Cross stitch				Backstitch	
■	310	▪	995	—	310
▫	321		996	—	321
	400		3705	—	blanc
	783	/	blanc		
o	972				

Stitch count 65h x 55w

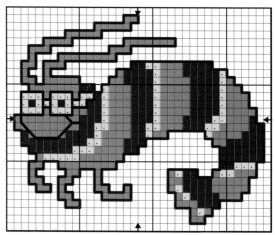

Shrimp
DMC stranded cotton

Cross stitch		Backstitch	
■	310	—	310
■	321	—	321
	740		
▪	818		

Stitch count 27h x 34w

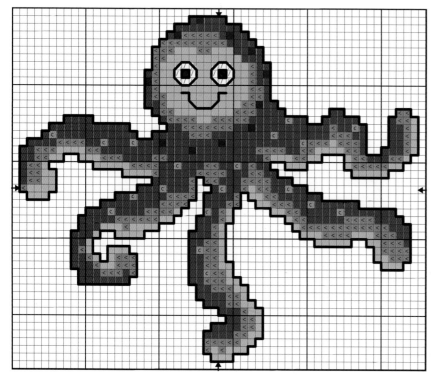

Octopus
DMC stranded cotton

Cross stitch				Backstitch	
	153	<	553	—	310
■	310	C	3708		
	552	/	blanc		

Stitch count 45h x 54w

View of the Lighthouse

For centuries, lighthouses have warned ships of treacherous coastlines and guided them to safe harbours. By night, the bright lights pointed out hazards on the coast and by day the distinctive buildings were used as markers to navigate along the coast. From simple beginnings with kerosene lamps that were tended by lighthouse keepers to today's automatic management, the lighthouse has been a beacon to travellers. Since lighthouses usually stand on the edge of the land overlooking the water, they offer a scenic spot to spend a little time reflecting on the power and beauty of the ocean, lake or river.

A favourite pastime of mine is visiting lighthouses when I travel. The lighthouse designs in this chapter are not specific buildings but they still reflect the calm security I feel when I see them. The lovely picture opposite shows a view of a lighthouse through a vintage-style porch, while two smaller lighthouse designs could be made up as pictures or as the handy doorstop shown below.

Day trips to a seaside village give us the opportunity to enjoy a leisurely lunch on a porch overlooking a scenic vista. Keep the memory alive by stitching this lovely picture.

View of the Lighthouse Picture

Few of us are lucky enough to wake each day to a view like this, unless of course you stitch this beautiful view of the lighthouse picture. A blue mount (mat) and brushed silver frame were used to echo the colour of the sky.

Stitch count
140h x 150w

Design size
25.5 x 27.2cm (10 x 10¾in)

You Will Need

White 14-count Aida
40.5cm (16in) square

Tapestry needle size 24–26

DMC stranded cotton (floss)
as listed in the chart key

Suitable picture frame

1 Prepare for work, referring to page 100 if necessary. Mark the centre of the fabric and centre of the chart on pages 90–93. Mount your fabric in an embroidery frame if you wish.

2 Start stitching from the centre of the chart and fabric and work over one block of Aida. Use two strands of stranded cotton for cross stitches and one strand for backstitches.

3 Once stitching is complete, press the work and then frame as desired (see page 102).

'A smooth sea never made
a skilled mariner.'
(Traditional saying)

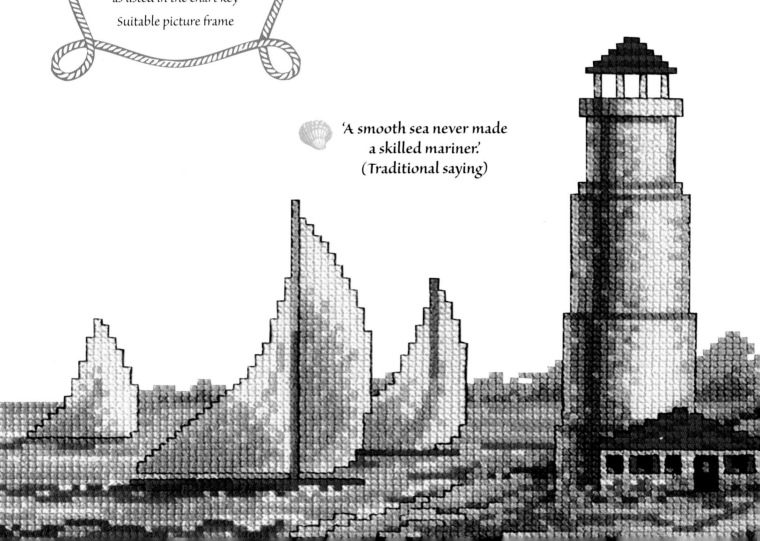

Doorstop

Just as a lighthouse stands tall with an important job to do, a weighted doorstop will prop the door when ocean breezes blow (see picture overleaf). Two sides of the doorstop are decorated with lighthouse designs.

1 Prepare for work, referring to page 100 if necessary. Mark the centre of the fabric and centre of the charts on pages 88 and 89. Mount your fabric in an embroidery frame if you wish.

2 Start stitching from the centre of the chart and fabric and work over one block of Aida. Use two strands of stranded cotton for cross stitches and one strand for backstitches.

3 Once stitching is complete, press the work. Cut two pieces of fusible fleece 2.5cm (1in) larger than the stitched area and fuse to the back of each of the embroideries (see page 102). Trim excess fabric to within five rows of the stitched area.

Making up the doorstop

4 To make the fabric box, cut out the following materials and then follow the instructions overleaf. Cut four pieces of striped fabric each 23 x 19cm (9 x 7½in), with stripes vertical. Cut two pieces of striped fabric each 19 x 19cm (7½ x 7½in). Cut two pieces of striped fabric each 16.5 x 5cm (6½ x 2in) for the handle. Cut four pieces of fusible fleece each 21.5 x 8cm (8½ x 7in). Cut two pieces of fusible fleece each 18 x 18cm (7 x 7in). Cut two pieces of fusible fleece each 15 x 3.5cm (6 x 1½in), for the handle.

Stitch count
(for each design)
78h x 58w

Design size
14 x 10.5cm (5½ x 4⅛in)

Finished size of doorstop
21.5 x 17.8 x 17.8cm (8½ x 7 x 7in)

You Will Need

White 14-count Aida, two 25.5cm (10in) squares

Tapestry needle size 24–26

DMC stranded cotton (floss) as listed in the chart key

Striped fabric 0.5m (½yd) (see step 4)

Fusible fleece 0.5m (½yd)

Gold braid trim 122cm (48in) long

Permanent fabric glue

Two decorative buttons

Polyfill stuffing

Several heavy stones

5 Centre the fusible fleece on each respective panel and fuse together according to the manufacturer's instructions. Sew the four vertical-striped side panels (the rectangles) together in a row, preferably by sewing machine and using a 6mm (¼in) seam. Place the lighthouse patches centrally on two of the panels and use permanent fabric glue to fix in place (see Fig 1).

6 Glue the braid all around the edges of the patches, beginning and ending at centre bottom. Allow to dry and then sew on a decorative button to cover the raw ends of the braid.

7 To make the handle, place the two smallest rectangles right sides together and sew the side seams and one end seam using a 6mm (¼in) seam allowance. Turn the handle right side out and tuck in the raw edge. Centre the handle on one square panel and topstitch each end of the handle to secure.

8 Sew the top and bottom panels to the four-panel unit (see Fig 2), leaving the last side panel open. Put the stones into the bottom of the fabric box. Fill the top part of the box with polyfill and then hand sew the side seam closed.

Fig 1
Sewing the four side panels together and attaching the embroidered patches

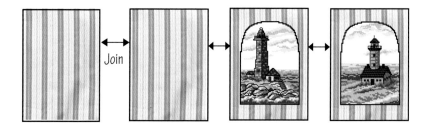

Fig 2
Attaching the top and base squares and sewing the fabric box together

Top square

Join

Join

Base square

'There is indeed, perhaps, no better way to hold communication with the sea than sitting in the sun on the veranda of a fisherman's café.'
(Joseph W. Banks)

Two lighthouse scenes decorate this handy doorstop but you could stitch each design twice, so views can be seen all around the doorstop. Alternatively, each design would make a lovely framed picture.

Lighthouse 1
DMC stranded cotton
Cross stitch   Backstitch

■ 310	~ 775	▨ 825	▨ 3325	▪ blanc	— 310
▨ 645	V 813	▨ 895	+ 3346
(647	/ 822	C 951	▨ 3348

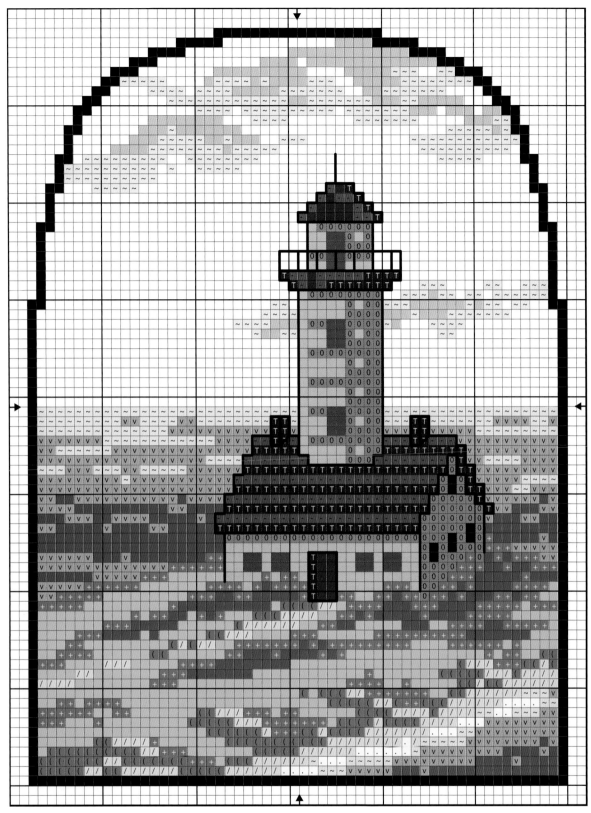

Lighthouse 2
DMC stranded cotton
Cross stitch

Backstitch

T 221	**0** 318	762	**/** 822	3325	**–** 3830	**—** 310
310	321	**~** 775	825	**+** 3346	**·** blanc	
317	**(** 647	**V** 813	895	3348		

View of the Lighthouse

DMC stranded cotton

Cross stitch

166	892
310	894
318	988
349	3013
413	3033
414	3078
415	3345
796	3363
798	3756
800	3862
809	3864
816	blanc

Backstitch

310
816
838
988

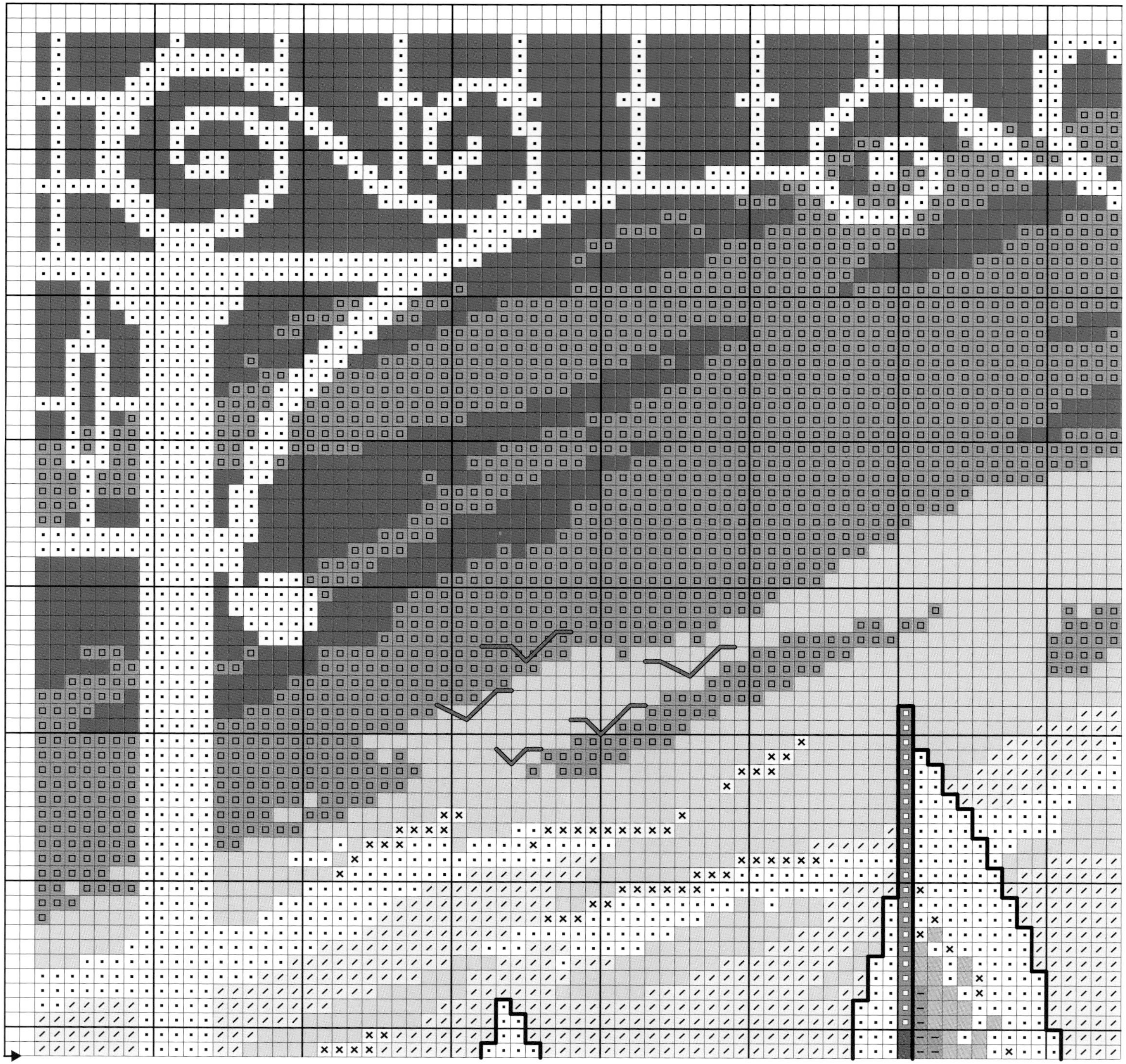

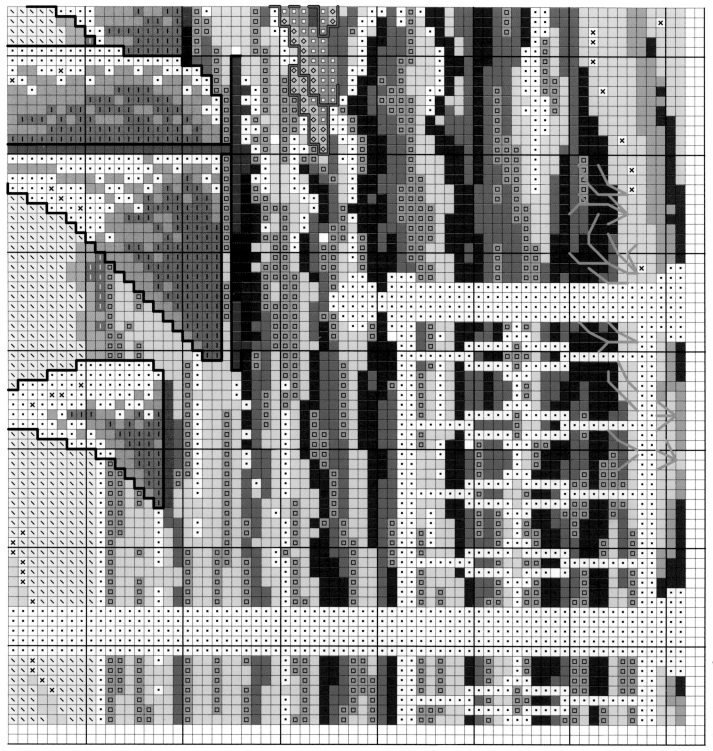

View of the Lighthouse

DMC stranded cotton

Cross stitch

	166	892
	310	894
	318	988
	349	3013
	413	3033
	414	3078
	415	3345
	796	3363
	798	3756
	800	3862
	809	3864
	816	blanc

Backstitch
- 310
- 816
- 838
- 988

Top Right

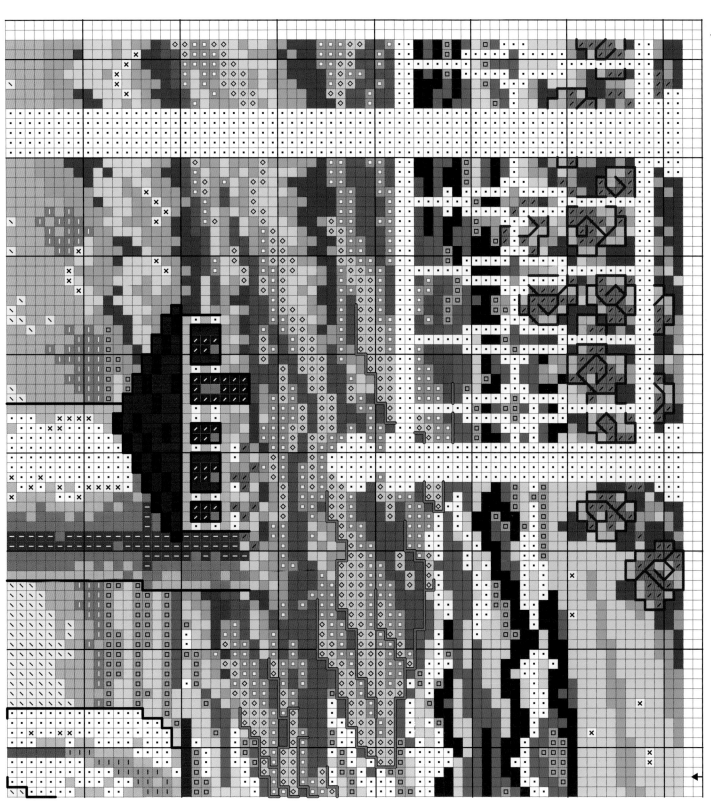

You and Me by the Sea

A day at the beach with your loved ones creates priceless memories. A long walk with your sweetheart along the edge of the water at sunset makes the heart grow fonder. Perhaps an early morning jog on the beach or an evening bonfire with a best friend is more your style. Whatever your preference, sharing a few hours by the sea with a special person is the perfect ending to a summer season.

A colourful wall quilt, stitched with love and finished with a vivid border, will make a unique gift for someone special. If time is short or if you prefer a simpler project, stitch the design on a pre-made pillow sham, as shown below, and decorate it with some seashell trim and pretty bows. Your hand-stitched creations, made from your heart, will certainly delight a family member or dear friend.

This sweet design is quite versatile: stitch it on a large-count fabric and it makes an impressive wall quilt or use a finer fabric to create a little cushion.

Wall Hanging

Select colourful batik fabrics that pick up the colours from a beach blanket or those seen in the summer sky to make your wall quilt dazzle with the warmth of the summer sun.

1 Prepare for work, referring to page 100 if necessary. Mark the centre of the fabric and centre of the chart on page 99. Mount your fabric in an embroidery frame if you wish.

2 Start stitching from the centre of the chart and fabric and work over two threads of evenweave. Use three strands of stranded cotton for full and three-quarter cross stitches and one strand for backstitches. Once stitching is complete, press.

Making up the hanging

3 Start by making the scrap border. Cut the batik fabric scraps into irregular rectangles about 9 x 6.3cm (3½ x 2½in). Lay the first rectangle on one end of one of the muslin strips, right side facing up. Lay the next rectangle, right sides together, over the first rectangle and sew the raw edge (see Fig 1 below). Flip the rectangle open and finger press. Continue adding rectangles to cover the muslin strip, arranging them at slight angles.

4 When the muslin strip is covered, press it and then place the border face down and trim excess fabric along each long edge. Repeat the stitch and flip procedure for the remaining three muslin strips.

Fig 1
Creating the fabric border using a stitch and flip technique on a strip of muslin

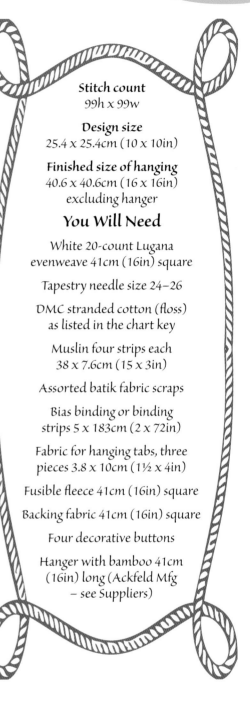

Irregular rectangles of fabric

Muslin strip   Stitch together

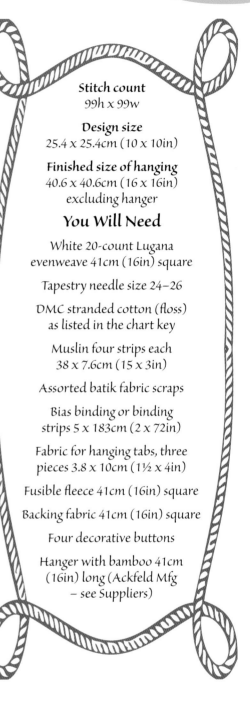

Stitch count
99h x 99w

Design size
25.4 x 25.4cm (10 x 10in)

Finished size of hanging
40.6 x 40.6cm (16 x 16in)
excluding hanger

You Will Need

White 20-count Lugana evenweave 41cm (16in) square

Tapestry needle size 24–26

DMC stranded cotton (floss) as listed in the chart key

Muslin four strips each 38 x 7.6cm (15 x 3in)

Assorted batik fabric scraps

Bias binding or binding strips 5 x 183cm (2 x 72in)

Fabric for hanging tabs, three pieces 3.8 x 10cm (1½ x 4in)

Fusible fleece 41cm (16in) square

Backing fabric 41cm (16in) square

Four decorative buttons

Hanger with bamboo 41cm (16in) long (Ackfeld Mfg – see Suppliers)

5 On the front of the work, measure a line 2.5cm (1in) away from the stitched area and mark lightly with a pencil. Place a border strip on the bottom edge of the work, right sides together and matching the long edge of the strip and the pencil line. Machine sew 6mm (¼in) in from the raw edge. Flip open the border. In a counter-clockwise manner, sew the remaining three borders around the work and then press.

6 With the work right side down, centre the fusible fleece on the back and then the backing fabric and fuse the layers together with a medium iron. Trim the edges if needed.

7 Cut the binding into four equal lengths. Pin a length to the bottom border, right sides together and matching raw edges, and sew in place. Fold the binding to the back of the work, tuck under the edge, pin and hand sew the binding to the backing. Repeat with the top binding and then the sides.

8 To make the hanging tabs, fold a 3.8 x 10cm (1½ x 4in) piece of fabric in thirds lengthways. Sew a seam lengthways to secure. Repeat to make two more tabs. Fold each tab in half and sew to the top edge on the back of the hanging.

9 Finish by sewing decorative buttons on each corner of the embroidery. Slip the dowel through the tabs and attach to the hanger.

'Love one another but make not a bondage of love; let it rather be a moving sea between the shores of your souls.'
(Kahil Gibran)

Cushion

On my grandmother's white wicker chair in my cottage bedroom are some fluffy striped pillows and this little stitched gem, bringing memories of wonderful days spent by the sea. After your design is stitched, add some funky trims to make the pillow sparkle with fun.

Stitch count
99h x 99w

Design size
18 x 18cm (7 x 7in)

You Will Need

Beige 14-count pre-made pillow sham (Charles Craft – see Suppliers)

Tapestry needle size 24–26

DMC stranded cotton (floss) as listed in the chart key

Sea beads trim 45cm (36in) (Expo International – see Suppliers)

Ribbon 6mm (¼in) wide x 91.5cm (36in) long

Cushion pad or pillow form

1 Prepare for work, referring to page 100 if necessary. Mark the centre of the fabric insert on the sham and centre of the chart opposite. If you prefer you could stitch the design on a 33cm (13in) square of 14-count Aida fabric.

2 Start stitching from the centre of the chart and fabric and work over one Aida block. Use two strands of stranded cotton for full and three-quarter cross stitches and one strand for backstitches. Once stitching is complete, press the work.

3 Hand sew the shell trim around the stitched area and then insert the cushion pad or make a pillow form following the instructions on page 102. If stitching the design on a square of Aida, make up into a cushion in a similar way to the lobster pillow on page 18. To finish, gather each corner of the cushion with a pretty ribbon and tie in a bow.

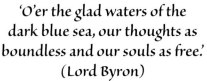
'O'er the glad waters of the dark blue sea, our thoughts as boundless and our souls as free.' (Lord Byron)

You and Me by the Sea
DMC stranded cotton
Cross stitch

					Backstitch
■ 321	+ 437	O 740	C 825	▦ 906	— 321
■ 414	▦ 444	▦ 762	V 827	▦ 3371	— 820
■ 434	▦ 739	▦ 813	■ 898	∕ blanc	— 3371

Materials, Techniques and Stitches

This brief section describes the materials and equipment you will need and the basic techniques and stitches used for the projects. Refer to Suppliers on page 104 for useful addresses.

Materials

Very few materials are required for cross stitch embroidery. Just needle, thread and fabric makes this a very portable craft.

Fabrics

The designs have been worked predominantly on a blockweave fabric called Aida. If you change the gauge (count) of the material, that is the number of holes per inch, then the size of the finished work will alter accordingly. Some designs have been stitched on evenweave linen and are worked over two fabric threads instead of one block.

Threads

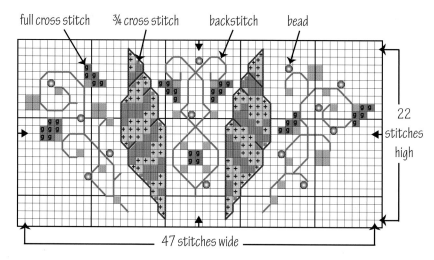

The projects have been stitched with DMC stranded embroidery cotton (floss) but you could match the colours to other thread ranges. The six-stranded skeins can easily be split into separate threads. The project instructions tell you how many strands to use.

Needles

Tapestry needles, available in different sizes, are used for cross stitch as they have a rounded point and do not snag fabric. A thinner, beading needle will be needed to attach seed beads.

Frames

Whether you use an embroidery frame to keep your fabric taut while stitching is a matter of personal preference. Generally speaking, working with a frame helps to keep the tension even and prevent distortion, while working without a frame is faster and less cumbersome. There are various types on the market – look in your local needlework shop.

Techniques

Cross stitch embroidery requires few techniques but your stitching will look its best if you follow the guidelines below.

Preparing the Fabric

Before starting work, check the design size given with each project and make sure that this is the size you require for your finished embroidery. Your fabric should be at least 5cm (2in) larger all the way round than the finished size of the stitching, to allow for making up. Before beginning to stitch, neaten the fabric edges either by hemming or zigzagging to prevent fraying as you work.

Finding the Fabric Centre

Marking the centre of the fabric is important, regardless of which direction you work from, in order to stitch the design centrally on the fabric. To find the centre, fold the fabric in half horizontally and then vertically, then tack (baste) along the folds. The centre point is where the two lines of tacking (basting) meet. This point on the fabric should correspond to the centre point on the chart. Remove these lines on completion of the work.

Calculating Design Size

Each project gives the stitch count and finished design size but if you want to work the design on fabric with a larger or smaller count, you will need to re-calculate the finished size.

To do this count the number of stitches in each direction on the chart (see Fig 1) and divide these numbers by the fabric count number. For example, a charted design with an overall size of 140 stitches high x 140 stitches wide ÷ 14-count = a design size of 10 x 10in (25.5 x 25.5cm). When working on Aida, work over one block. Working on evenweave usually means working over two fabric threads, so divide the fabric count by two before you start calculating.

Using Charts and Keys

The charts in this book are easy to work from. Each square on the chart represents one stitch. Each coloured square, or coloured square with a symbol, represents a thread colour, with the code number given in the chart key. Some designs use fractional stitches (three-quarter stitches) to give more definition to the design and these are shown by little squares (see Fig 1). Solid coloured lines show where backstitches or long stitches are to be worked.

full cross stitch ¾ cross stitch backstitch bead

22 stitches high

47 stitches wide

Fig 1
Working out the stitch count of a chart. The stitches are also identified here

French knots are shown by coloured circles. Larger coloured circles indicate beads. Each complete chart has arrows at the side to show the centre point, which you could mark with a pen. Where charts are split over several pages, the key is repeated. For your own use, you could colour photocopy and enlarge charts, taping the parts together.

Starting and Finishing Stitching

Avoid using knots when starting and finishing as this will make your work lumpy when mounted. Instead, bring the needle up at the start of the first stitch, leaving a 'tail' of about 2.5cm (1in) at the back. Secure the tail by working the first few stitches over it. Start new threads by first passing the needle through several stitches on the back of the work.

To finish off thread, pass the needle through some nearby stitches on the wrong side of the work, then cut the thread off, close to the fabric.

Washing and Pressing

If you need to wash your finished embroidery, first make sure the stranded cottons are colourfast by washing them in tepid water and mild soap. Rinse well and lay out flat to dry completely before stitching. Wash completed embroideries in the same way. Iron immediately after washing on a medium setting, covering the ironing board with a thick layer of towelling. Place the stitching right side down and press gently.

Stitches

Backstitch

Backstitches are used to give definition to parts of a design and to outline areas. Many charts used different coloured backstitches. Follow the diagram below, bringing the needle up at 1 and down at 2, up again at 3 and down at 4 and so on. Work backstitches after the cross stitches for a neater finish.

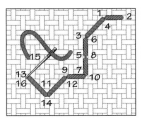

Fig 2 Working backstitch

Cross Stitch

A cross stitch can be worked singly (Fig 3a) or a number of half stitches can be sewn in a line and completed on the return journey (Fig 3b).

To make a cross stitch over one block of Aida, bring the needle up through the fabric at the bottom left side of the stitch (number 1 on Fig 3a) and cross diagonally to the top right corner (2). Push the needle through the hole and bring up through the bottom right corner (3), crossing the fabric diagonally to the top left corner to finish the stitch (4). To work the next stitch, come up through the bottom left corner of the first stitch and repeat the steps above.

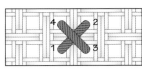

Fig 3a Working a single cross stitch

To work a line of cross stitches, stitch the first part of the stitch as above and repeat these half cross stitches along the row. Complete the crosses on the way back. Always finish the cross stitch with the top stitches lying in the same diagonal direction.

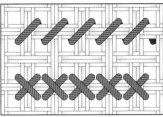

Fig 3b Working cross stitch in two journeys

Three-quarter Cross Stitch

Three-quarter cross stitches give more detail to a design and can create the illusion of curves. They are shown by a small square within a square on the charts. These stitches are easier to work on evenweave fabric than Aida. To work on Aida follow the diagram below, first working a half cross stitch and then making a quarter stitch from the corner into the centre, piercing the fabric if working on Aida.

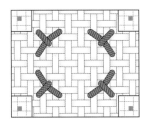

Fig 4 Working three-quarter cross stitch

Long Stitch

This is used for some of the lettering and other details throughout the book. Simply work a long, straight stitch starting and finishing at the points indicated on the chart.

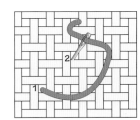

Fig 5 Working a long stitch

Attaching Beads

Adding beads will bring sparkle and texture to a cross stitch embroidery. Attach seed beads using ordinary sewing thread which matches the fabric colour and a beading needle or very fine 'sharp' needle and a half or whole cross stitch.

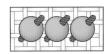

Fig 6 Attaching beads

Making Up

The embroideries in this book are very versatile and can be made up in many ways. Generally, making up is included with projects but some general techniques are described here.

Using Fusible Products

Iron-on interfacing and fusible fleece can be used to stiffen and stabilize your cross stitch embroidery and allow the edges to be cut without fraying. Adhesive webbing is available as single-sided and double-sided, i.e., with glue on one side or both, allowing you to fuse the embroidery to another fabric, which means you can use your cross stitch to decorate many ready-made items. Read the manufacturer's instructions before using these products as they vary slightly. Cut the interfacing or webbing to size and fuse it to the back of the finished embroidery with a medium iron, placing the embroidery face down into some thick towels.

Making Up as a Patch

When a small motif is made up as a patch, it may be applied to various surfaces. Iron the fusible interfacing or fleece on to the back of the embroidery and then trim the excess fabric around the stitched area. The fusible backing prevents the fabric threads from unravelling. The patch may be glued to a home accessory item or stitched to a wearable or soft surface. For a sleek, professional finish, cover the edges of the patch with a trimming such as ric-rac braid.

Making Up into a Card

Many of the designs would make lovely greetings cards. You will need: a ready-made card mount (aperture to fit embroidery) and craft glue or double-sided tape.

1 Trim the edges of the embroidery to fit the card. Apply a thin coat of glue or a piece of double-sided tape to the inside of the card opening. (Note: some cards already have this tape in place.)

2 Position the embroidery, checking the stitching is central, and press down firmly. Fold the spare flap inside, sticking or gluing it in place.

Making Up as a Framed Picture

Many of the designs in this book make wonderful framed pictures. For a polished finish, with a wider choice of mounts and frames, you could take your work to a professional framer. To frame work yourself you will need: a picture frame (aperture size to fit embroidery), a piece of foamcore board or heavyweight card slightly smaller than the frame, straight pins and adhesive tape or a staple gun.

1 Iron your embroidery and trim the edges if necessary. Centre the embroidery on the foamcore board or thick card. Fold the edges of the embroidery to the back and push the straight pins into the sides of the foamcore to anchor the embroidery into position. Use adhesive tape or a staple gun to fix the edges of the fabric in place.

2 Insert the picture into the frame and secure the back with adhesive tape or staples.

Making a Pillow Form

Pillows and cushions will have a smooth, professional look when a separate poly-filled form is inserted. You will need lining fabric and polyester filling (polyfill).

1 After your embroidered pillow is constructed, measure it. Using a lining fabric, make another pillow the same size as the embroidered pillow. Cut two squares of lining fabric, place right sides together and sew around the edges leaving a gap for turning through.

2 Turn the lining bag right side out, stuff with polyester filling (polyfill) and sew the opening closed. Stuff this form inside the embroidered pillow and finish the edges of the pillow as desired.

Attaching Heat-set Crystals

After your stitching is complete you can easily add a sparkling touch to your projects with heat-set crystals. You will need a special wand with a tip that heats an individual crystal. The tip will lift the crystal from your work surface and heat the adhesive that is on the back of the crystal. You may then touch the crystal to the embroidery, where it will stick as it cools down. An alternate method of applying crystals is to dot the back of the crystal with tacky glue and place it on the embroidery.

Bunting Templates (full size)

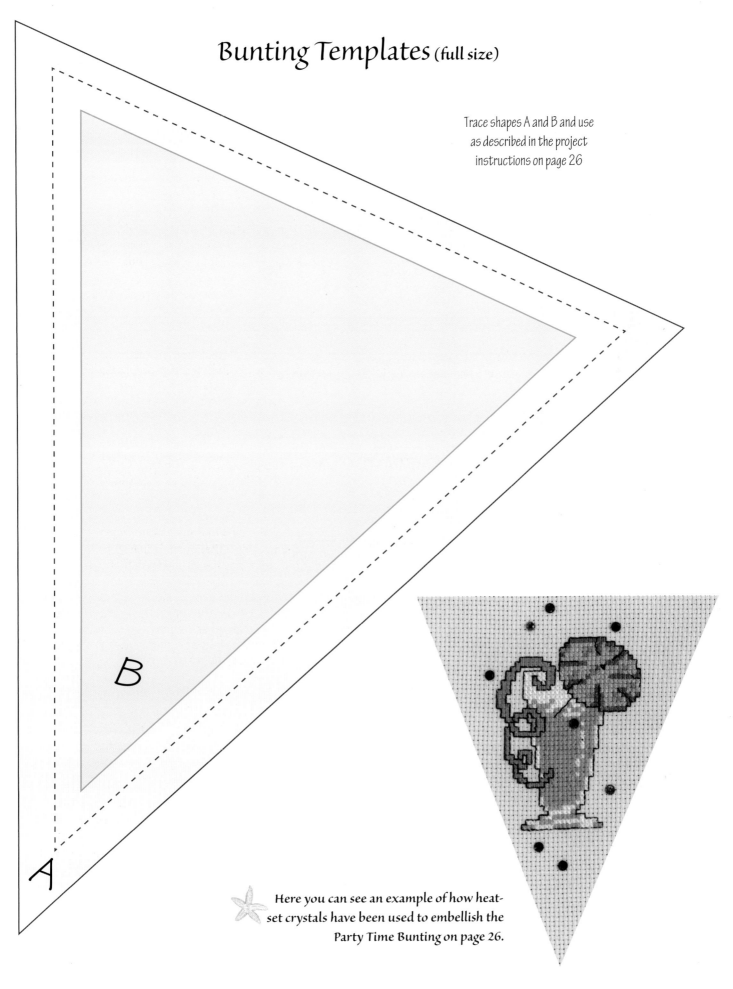

Trace shapes A and B and use
as described in the project
instructions on page 26

B

A

Here you can see an example of how heat-
set crystals have been used to embellish the
Party Time Bunting on page 26.

Suppliers

UK

Coats Crafts UK
PO Box 22, Lingfield Estate,
McMullen Road, Darlington,
County Durham DL1 1YQ
Tel: 01325 365457 (for a list of stockists)
For Anchor stranded cotton (floss) and other embroidery supplies. Coats also supply some Charles Craft products

DMC Creative World
1st Floor Compass Building, Feldspar Close,
Enderby, Leicestershire, LE19 4SD
Tel: 0116 275 4000
Fax: 0116 275 4020
www.dmccreative.co.uk
For stranded cotton (floss), fabrics and other embroidery supplies

Framecraft Miniatures Ltd.
Unit 3, Isis House, Linden Road,
Brownhills, Walsall, West
Midlands WS8 7BW
Tel: 01543 373 076
Fax: 01543 453 154
www.framecraft.com
For pre-finished items with cross stitch inserts
USA Distributor: Anne Brinkley Designs Inc.
3895B N Oracle Rd, Tuscon,
AZ 85705, USA
Tel: 520 888 1462
Fax: 520 888 1483

Madeira Threads (UK) Ltd.
PO Box 6, Thirsk, North Yorkshire
YO7 3YX
Tel: 01845 524880
Email: info@madeira.co.uk
www.madeira.co.uk
For Madeira stranded cotton (floss) and other embroidery supplies

USA

Ackfeld Manufacturing
PO Box 539, Reeds Spring, MO 65737
Tel: 1-888-272-3135
www.ackfeldwire.com
For the hanger on page 96 (Memories 16in)

Charles Craft Inc.
PO Box 1049, Laurinburg, NC 28353
Tel: 910 844 3521
Email: ccraft@carolina.net
www.charlescraft.com
For cross stitch fabrics and pre-finished items, including ecru Maxton Guest Towel page 40 (code VT-6910-5708-EA), HomeDec Pillow Sham page 98 (code AF-7312-6750-EA) and tote page 75 (code TG-2091-5830-EA)

Expo International Inc.
5631 Braxton Drive, Houston, TX 77036
Tel: 1-800-542-4367
www.expointl.com
For shell trim used on the cushion on page 98

Kandi Corp.
PO Box 8345, Clearwater, Florida 33758
Tel: 1-800-985-2634 or 727-669-8000
www.kandicorp.com
For embellishments including heat-set crystals

Sudberry House
PO Box 895, Old Lyme, CT 06371
Tel: 860 739 6951
Email: sales@sudberry.com
www.sudberry.com
For quality wooden products for displaying needlework, including the black tray on page 66 (code #68007)

Wichelt Imports
N162 Hwy 35, Stoddard, WI 54658
Tel: 800 356 9516
Fax: 608 788 6040
www.wichelt.com
For Mill Hill beads, buttons and cross stitch fabrics

Zweigart/Joan Toggit Ltd.
262 Old Brunswick Road, Suite E,
Piscataway, NJ 08854-3756
Tel: 732 562 8888
Email: info@zweigart.com
www.zweigart.com
For a large selection of cross stitch fabrics

Acknowledgments

There are so many people who work behind the scenes to make my designs look good. I'd like to thank my commissioning editor, Cheryl Brown, for her vision and guidance through the entire book design process. Many thanks to Lin Clements, my editor, for her patience to blend my art, my words and my seaside dreams together to craft a truly lovely book. Credits go to Charly Bailey and Eleanor Stafford for their unique layouts, to Bethany Dymond for her organizing skills, to Kate Nicholson for fine-tuning my work and to the fantastic photographers, Kim Sayer and Karl Adamson, for their exquisite photos. Along with the marketing staff, everyone has been wonderful to work with as our thoughts and projects travelled across the big blue sea.

My sincerest thanks to my stitchers, Susan Chamis, Anita Pidgeon, Lois Schultz and Robyn Purta, for their excellent work, comments and pleasant conversations, which made each charted project come to sparkling life.

Several manufacturers have supplied me with their quality products and thanks go to: Kreinik for metallic threads (www.kreinik.com); Airtex for poly-fill and batting (www.airtex.com); Havel's for scissors (www.havels.com); Art Glitter for glitter and fabric glue (www.artglitter.com); Beacon Adhesives for tacky glue (www.beaconcreates.com); East Side Mouldings for frames (www.eastsidemouldings.com); Thermoweb Adhesives for fusible adhesives (www.thermoweb.com) and K&Company for stickers and decorative papers (www.kandcompany.com).

Finally, my deepest thank you is to my husband, Al, who has encouraged me and allowed me to pursue my dreams for all my working years. Living with scraps of fabric scattered about the house, needles in the sofa and stacks of projects cluttering the house, Al is a very special person that I love to spend time with, by the sea.

About the Author

Ursula Michael has worked as a professional needlework designer for over 20 years. Her cross stitch patterns have delighted stitchers in numerous magazines, as kits, in books and on products manufactured for embroidery. Ursula strives to create designs that are bright and cheery, heartfelt, inspiring and fun to stitch. Besides cross stitch, Ursula designs appliqué quilts, motifs for machine embroidery and sewing crafts. With threads and fibres in hand, she has woven her motifs into the hearts of many stitchers. Living on a coastal island in southern New England, USA has inspired Ursula to create this lovely book of seaside designs.

Index